JACQUELINE JOHNSON

SECRETS OF THE EARTH REVEALED

SECRETS OF THE EARTH REVEALED

Secrets of the Earth, Revealed
Published by Jacqueline Johnson
Printed in the United States of America

ISBN 979-8-9907820-6-8 E-book
ISBN 979-8-9907820-9-9 Audio book
ISBN 979-8-9907820-5-1 Softcover
ISBN 979-8-9907820-3-7 Hardcover

This book is dedicated to a man who has chosen to serve me in the sweetest, kindest, and most thoughtful ways.
My son, Joune Fraser.

CONTENTS

PROLOGUE

The greatest mystery of all time has not yet been solved, or has it? Everyone has asked the question, searching for the answers, sometimes in places where the answers cannot be found.

Ingeniously, we invented *science* and shrouded it in formulas and mathematical theories understood only by the chosen few. These creative minds of exceptional intellectual brilliance concocted theories to answer the question but came up short as their stories kept evolving.

The truth is, every question has an answer, or its creative genius would fail. If fishes are created to live in water, then water must be provided, or there would be no fish. If birds are created to fly, they must be given wings, or their purpose would fail. Creation, at its core, is guided by answers and solutions so that the intended purpose of the Creator can be fulfilled.

Creation would collapse and life would be a bumbling failure if every question did not have an inbuilt answer. Every disease has its cure, every star has a name, light has a source, and man—where did he come from?

THE SACRIFICE

The he peaceful bliss of Heaven was perfectly disrupted: the ambiance, the splendor—nothing remained the same. One-third of the angels, along with their leader, were booted out on the grounds of treachery, but Satan refused to accept defeat. His blood was churning with the lava of revenge as he claimed ownership of everyone who did not fight in the battle. He wanted the third of the angels who did not enlist in the war to also be labeled traitors. In so doing, they too would be kicked out of Heaven to feel the pangs of separation from God.

Satan knew that the most valuable possession of God is His created being. He saw the pain in God's heart as he fought for God's throne, but he would not rest until he ripped God's heart open with his knife of jealousy. He did not get the throne, but it was possible that he could argue for God to kick out those who did not defend Him. There was still more damage to be done. He must make the case to steal, then kill and destroy any created being who did not join him in the fight against God, so they too would join him in the flames of eternal hell.

From clear across the abyss, he began to yell with his nauseating fumes of venom. "If they did not fight for You, why do You think they love You? It is only a matter of time before they rise up, just as I did, and overthrow Your weakness. You think You are being kind and just, but that is Your weakness. No one wants that—we are indestructible, we are strong, we don't need Your weakness. They belong to me; we are cut from the same cloth, and we hate You. If You don't believe me, put them to the test. God, put them to the test. Give them the chance to prove that they are dedicated to You."

"Some God You are, and that Son You have chosen, He is just like them. He stood by and watched as Michael almost got slaughtered by my sword. He deserves to die. Your kingdom is full of a bunch of no-good, weak, spineless betrayers. All You have to do is put them to the test. Don't take my word for it; put them to the test. If they love You, they will pass the test."

"By the way, pull your protection. I don't have your protection, and my generals do not have Your protection. Why should they? Make it a fair fight; make it fair, YWHY. The only thing You can give them in this fight is knowledge. You can only tell them that You exist, then let them choose. I will show them my hand, my power, my ability to give them all their little hearts' desire, and every one of them will hate Your guts."

"You weak image of a God. Your Kingdom is worth nothing. No one loves You, we will all curse You to Your face and willingly go to Hell. You are worth nothing, and I will prove it. I will tell them how horrible You are. I will tell them that all You represent are lies and pain. I will take what You have done to me and plaster it all over Your stainless image. When I am done, You will be sorry You did not choose me to become Your Only Begotten Son."

"From this day on, you will be called *Satan the Accuser*; and just as you have described your evil intentions, you will be called *Devil*. I will entertain your offer; it seems reasonable. Here are the terms. You will retain your beauty; I have given that to you as a gift and I will not take it from you. You will also retain your gift of musical ingenuity and your given Heavenly name, *Lucifer*. I will create a place for this which you have proposed to play out, and I will give you a season to prove your theory. I will call the place *Earth*, and I will call the season *Time*."

"The knowledge I will give to My children on the Earth will be limited to My existence and My love. I will remove their spiritual abilities and make them subjects of the Earth who cannot enter Heaven in their physical form. In the Earth, they too will have a season or a limited time to remain in it. This will be the number of days they are given to make the choice of where they will spend their eternal life."

"Gabriel, take notes, please. We will design a trail of secured written information for My sons to read while on Earth. We will call this written information *The Word*. As they look upon The Word, it will enter into their souls and they will know the entire truth deep within their hearts. The truth will set them free from the grip of the Devil and will be the entryway back to Heaven. Those who do not pursue The Word will live life from the highs and lows of their emotions. Some will choose to lift their eyes and look upon and become The Word; they will live life with purpose."

"Father, Father, please, this is an unpredictable deal. We could lose all our brethren. Please, give me permission to shut the mouth of this filthy dragon. I promise, You will never hear the scorn of his disrespect again." Michael was on alert, standing beside the Lord, his sword drawn, waiting for the signal to attack the beast. Wasn't it enough that the evil had desecrated the Father's throne? Wasn't that enough? As God's Warrior General, it was his privilege to protect the Father, the Son, and all of Heaven. He was the tallest and strongest of them all, head to shoulder taller than all. That was a gift for which he was thankful, and he showed his gratitude through his fierce defense of God. "I am at Your command, Most High. Let me finish him off, let me remove his existence completely. He does not deserve to exist. Father, my troops are ready, we will defend Your honor, and we will not perish."

"This will be his only redemption, and My children who did not fight will prove their love. I will allow it."

"We submit to You my God, with all our hearts. Show us the plan." Michael stepped back, bowing to the Lord.

"My children will enter the Earth without any knowledge of the joys of Heaven or who I Am. I will only reveal to them My name and My word; that will be enough. Before we proceed, I will need a sacrifice to cleanse Heaven of the treachery of this war. It will be a sacrifice great enough to pay for My children who did not fight for My honor. A sacrifice to silence the Accuser so he will never be able to point a finger of accusation at My children again."

"Father, we know this rebellion is a rejection of Your decision to choose Me as Your Son. I will become Your sacrifice. It will be My offering to prove My love for You, My God." Jesus fell to His knees and leaned against the feet of His Father. He was a mild-mannered, gentle soul. God had poured every treasure of Heaven into Him, but He wore His power so well, no one could really tell. "You chose Me to become Your Only Begotten Son, and I choose to be slain as Your sacrifice of love: and let it be done on the Earth as it will be in Heaven."

"It is done. Put the plans in place and let us begin. The slaughter of My Son will be first, then we will create the Earth."

"Adam, you will be My first choice into the Earth. I will place My DNA in you, and from you will be born all My children who enter the Earth."

"Father, can I be first?" Enoch was a rough, burly warrior whose words carried a lot of weight. "I will honor Your Name before Your enemy, and I will fight to protect all who come through me."

"Father, Enoch and I have been talking: we want to make things right." Able was a tiny thing, always bubbling with laughter and always finding a gift to share with others. He got his name because he was always able to share. Some called him the 'Golden Giver'. "We did not fight because we were afraid. The war was brutal: it was not because we did not love You, but because we were terribly afraid. If You allow Enoch to be first, I will be his first son. We are committed to You and we know we will never fail You, never again."

"Able, My son, I know you won't. You will love Me unto death, but My vision for the Earth is different. I know the sons who are committed to Me. Enoch, you will be one of the firsts, but not the first."

A line had begun to form. Humbled and broken, they came out of hiding, weeping before the Lord.

Abraham had tears in his eyes, "As an archangel, My Lord, I can tell You that many of us who did not fight are dedicated to Your Majesty. We were frightened by the war. My Lord, it was a reign of terror such as could not be imagined. The plot was not just to take Your throne, but to destroy the purity and beauty of this place. Those who opposed the evil were to be destroyed instantly. We tried to escape for our lives. We beg Your pardon, Father, with all our hearts; and so I ask that You allow me to lead the charge of Your honor on the Earth. Let me be a father to nations, a father who will lead by example. I want to be a father like You, my God."

"Abraham, that is an excellent request. It is granted. From your loins will proceed a lineage to whom I will grant direct access to My heart. Your lineage will be My own special people. To confirm My word, I will send My Only Begotten Son to the Earth through you, that My honor may rest upon you."

"My Father, please forgive me; I failed You as well, but I promise I will not fail You again. I will take the punishment of going to the Earth; all I ask is that You make me a leader of millions so I can show them who You are. I have served in Your Presence, so many times as a communicator of Your heart, I do not know why I did not enter the fight. Father, please forgive me. Let my name, *Moses*, be a name in the Earth where every man will know how much I love you."

Father, I too am broken over my decision to run and hide. I know Your love for me is strong, You have called me Your beloved, and I cherish the moments I sit at Your feet with the heavenly harp and play for You. I will go down as well. I only ask that You give me the role of protecting Your Only Begotten Son, and His Name, and His legacy on the Earth. Let me stand in the gap and take on His pain; let me intercede for Him in travail, that He will not carry the sacrifice of the brutal slaughter alone. I give myself to be betrayed, and hunted, and wounded unto death for Christ. Father, I will take on the pains of death for Your first beloved."

"David, your request is granted."

"May I be chosen to bring Him into the Earth? Father, I did not fight because I too was afraid, but I love You with all my heart. I want to be the one who nurtures and brings Him up in Your knowledge and wisdom. That is my gift, Father, I am a nurturer; I will care for Your son with the sweetest of tenderness."

"Mary, I have poured My gentleness into your soul, but in the Earth, it will be pierced with the sword of pain."

"Well then, it is done."

"My God, I too need to confess, I too must repent before You." The heavy sobs were drowning out His words. "I must admit I was drawn into the lie that You were a weak God and must be overthrown. With just a sliver of force, those words entered my soul, but when I saw the battle, I resisted the force and ran into hiding. Oh God..." Saul was weeping so hard that God had to touch his heart to keep it from exploding. "Oh God, I repent... I repent. Ohhh... God... I truly repent. Please let me suffer for Your name's sake. Please let me be whipped and... and stoned... and even crucified so that Your son's name be exalted. Do all You will, just let me suffer for You and Your Son Jesus Christ."

Tears were everywhere. Lucifer's angels were repenting as well. Many of them were in tears. Adolf threw himself on the ground and screamed, shrieking in pain. He pulled his sword and would have punctured his heart, but Lucifer snatched it. Lucifer pulled out his weapon and wielded it in the air while flames of fire gushed from his mouth.

"Dare any of you cave in, dare any of you. I will punish you so severely; I will chain you in darkness and torture you with the fire of my power. You are mine, and you will remain mine."

Once he saw he had gained the respect of the masses, he walked over to the whimpering Adolf. With his 'Hit-left' right hook, Lucifer bludgeoned the left eye of the one he had chosen to be his personal deputy during the war. The blow sent an instant shock to the brain, leaving poor Adolf permanently mentally damaged. Then he looked at the crowd, "Who's next?"

God stood from His throne. "My Son is next. You may proceed to the slaughter. The holy sacrifice will be the initiation of this plan. Saints, gather together and witness the brutality of the evil one; it must be done."

THE GARDEN PARTY

What a fine garden, and oh, the colors! God had taken the blackness of the deep and transformed it into life. Every created thing had that life-giving effect within to keep on nourishing itself. However, all you had to do was look a little closer to realize everything was programmed to die.

Lucifer strutted up and down, admiring all he saw, taking note of every detail, and conspiring in his heart to tear it down. After all, he was the mastermind behind it all. Pride welled up in his heart like an oversized balloon waiting to pop. God was indeed generous to consent to his plan; yes, this was his plan, and look at how splendid it turned out. How foolish! Though God could see through the evil intent of his heart, God still allowed the plan to prevail. That is the epitome of weakness. Then, as if He approved of the evil intent, God took the plan and decorated it with His heart. If he were God, he would have made a botched, dried-up piece of junk. No, not God. His love and kindness will be His demise. Lucifer vowed to spin that tale and make Him sorry.

The garden was indeed ready. In the midst of it, God had cast a tree, a tree from which Lucifer could perch and watch the details of Earth unfold. Adam was sent down first—that fool. Lucifer narrowly missed the opportunity to get him on his team during the fight, he could not afford to miss this time as this was his last shot at true power. He pondered the use of force, but that was not guaranteed. He needed something more subtle, something charming and sweet to the taste. It had to be something Adam desired, and it had to be a mind game, because if he got control of the mind he would own him for life, and his children, and his inheritance. That was it, that was the perfect plan; get Adam to think like Lucifer and not like God. As he imagined the whole Earth being turned over to him, the smell of power made his body tremble. He calmed himself. Instead of executing the plan immediately, he must go into hiding to examine and re-examine the details. He vowed on the life of his soul, never to fail this one.

God made several trips to help Adam get settled in the garden, but it was not long before Adam began asking for a companion. God kept telling him it was not a wise idea, he needed to become familiar with the Earth first, as it possessed secrets that could prove dangerous. Lately, the conversation seemed to circle back to the same request.

"When are You going to give me someone I can talk with? When You leave, it becomes awfully lonely."

Again, God assured him that there were things he needed to understand about himself and his environment before the influence of another. Adam could not understand how the sweetness of intimacy could upset his world and he pleaded with God for a companion.

God complied, and the first surgery was done. Adam woke up to find this gorgeous beauty by his side. He told God, "You don't need to visit as often anymore; in fact, give us time to bond."

The garden came alive. Perfection was perfected with this gorgeous woman who was pulled out of his side. The animals competed for her attention by bringing her fruits and leaves every day. The Chimps and the Chipmunks formed a band and sounded out beats for her while Adam taught her to dance. The garden was filled with giggles and laughter as the man and the woman enjoyed the bliss of Earth. At night, they would huddle together on the plush grass, and holding each other tightly, they would fall deep into sleep. Mornings were amazing. Adam used his mornings to explore and speak to the land. At times, he would take Eve over to Havilah and show her the gold, the bdellium, and the onyx stones. From there, he would travel to Ethiopia to ensure all the treasures around him were alive and beautiful.

As the sun warmed the land, it was time to play, and they would race through the jungles on horseback. One of their favorite games was called 'Hide and Seek'. Lion liked to be the judge, he would set rules for the games and most of his rules avoided playing with any of the sea creatures. One day, in the midst of Hide and Seek, Snake made the rule that Adam would ride out to the ocean and wait until Sun was low before he came looking for Eve. As they searched for a place to hide, Snake took her to the tree in the midst of the garden.

"I don't want to play here," she said.

"Why, it's the perfect place. Adam will never find us. He will never look for us here because God told us not to come near this tree."

"No, He told us not to eat of the tree, so we decided not to even come near the thing."

"I wonder why God does not want us to eat of it?"

"Isn't that irrelevant? We have every other tree to eat from; we don't need its fruit."

"Eve, have you ever looked at the tree? It has something that no other tree has. Come, let me show you. Come on! I went looking yesterday, and I found that when you come into its presence, it changes you; you become like God."

"Like God?"

"Yes, God left His touch on the tree, and when we come close to it something inside us begins to change. I believe when we eat its fruit, we will no longer have to live in this garden, but we will be able to go to the place where God lives, and we will become like God."

"Snake, stop. Stop! Eve, come with me."

Snake almost popped out of his skin. "Adam, where did you come from? I thought you were gone to the ocean."

"Eve, come with me; this is wrong. I know God. If He tells us not to eat of the tree, we need not question His wisdom, we just trust."

"Adam, yesterday I went to the tree, and as I talked with it, it told me something you and Eve do not know. It told me of a time when we all lived in Heaven with God, but now, we are kicked out of God's Presence to be punished. As beautiful as this garden of Earth is, it is a garden of punishment. Then the tree gave me its fruit, and I ate. Look, look in my belly—there is a river of life in me. Tree told me that if I do not eat its fruit, it will only be a matter of time before I die; but if I eat, I will become a god and live forever. I never knew God would hide these secrets from us."

Snake's lips were quivering as he presented the fruit to Eve, all the while cautiously eyeing Adam. "Here, Eve, take, eat, and live forever."

Eve looked at Adam, the glint of mischief twirling in her eyes.

Adam turned his head. "I trust God. I trust God more than anything, and I refuse to disobey Him."

Eve reached out and plucked a fruit from the tree. Adam just stared in disbelief, frozen in place, wanting to resist but feeling powerless. What was this? He knew it was wrong, but there was a certain force in the air that made the wrong acceptable. No, that was not it, the force made him like a robot. It was as if he was in the presence of a power that could make him go against his will—do something that was deadly. He could see death coming, but the power prevented him from resisting.

Eve was eating, and he could see her soul changing. The juices of the fruit were turning her insides deathly black, and she could see it, but the enjoyment of the fruit was more powerful than the death. He wanted to snatch it away from her, but instead, he reached out and took it from her hand and began enjoying its juices.

Nothing in the garden tasted as good. It shocked his senses. His entire body was lit with a fire of pleasure so intense he felt like bursting; then slowly, it felt like needles of anguish were breaking open inside. He looked at Eve and her smile was strange—an evil grin mixed with fear, and pain, and shame.

Snake had climbed to the top of the tree, almost out of sight. Many of the animals had gathered, staring in shock and disbelief. He looked at them and looked around, he knew the truth now, he had been trapped—trapped in a death-vise. He must get away, far away, but his mind was not making sense. Eve, her eyes were hollow and empty: and her soul, her soul was struggling with a hand, the hand of fate. Adam grabbed her, but it got her before he did. It swallowed her mind first and, with one invisible swoop, her soul was gone. He took her hand, they had to hide from it, run far away and hide.

THE MYSTERY OF MAN

To legitimize Heaven, the garden of Eden, and all the activities before the beginning of time, there must first be proof that God is real. Within that context, there must also be evidence that man is a spirit who came from God and will return to God. The verdict of this court must be conclusive and without bias or speculation, or man will return to the weakness of those who have no hope. The case for God and eternal life must be proven once and for all.

Eternal life starts here and now with every decision man makes in the Earth. However, the trend of the present culture disrupts any talk of eternity and focuses instead on the need for immediate gratification. Still, there is an unrest stirring in the heart of man, demanding change. He is becoming agitated because life is supposed to get better with age, not worse. He has pursued knowledge, and the arts, and technology, and religion, and fame; man has chased every dream in his soul, but nothing has quieted the nagging questions of his heart. The Earth is now in the twilight of its years, and the age-old questions that have plagued man's mind, producing sleepless nights, must be answered without delay.

"Who am I, where did I come from, and why am I here? What is the meaning of life?"

In pursuit of the answer, he enslaves himself to achievements, attempting to be greater than his fellow man. After the accolades and showers of praise, emptiness rises to new levels and sends him on the chase for more. To silence the noise, he craves comfort, and invents luxuries to experience happiness, only to find that comforts do not contain lasting joy.

He searches out knowledge, then labels it as hallmarks of truth. Given time, competition mocks his findings, and soon his research is tossed aside for newer inventions. Slowly, he learns that it is out of his realm to create truth. He finds that the standards of truth do not change, they are spiritual and eternal concepts built into the mechanics of life. It means, that which truly satisfies the soul, cannot be found in the expressions of man's imagination; it is outside the realm of his capacity. It may just be that he has to silence the noise and ask the questions again.

What is man's role in the grand scheme of life? Is man simply an angel sent into the Earth to make the choice for his eternal home? If God is the source of life, how can man truly know that He exists? This place called Earth, is it just a venue selected to prepare the souls of men for eternity?

The mystery of man is the inner workings of his being, which he struggles to define. At some point in life, every man struggles within himself to know himself. He can locate his heart, but he needs to find his soul. He knows he is a spirit because his thoughts and imaginations communicate on a higher level; yet all this beauty needs to be explained. During these days of struggle, God is closest to his heart, and speaks with sweet, gentle conversations to man. In these moments, man often finds himself alone while he converses with the thoughts in his head. This is the place where dreams are born and where he learns to honor God.

As a young boy called to be a prophet of God, Jeremiah struggled to find himself and to define the path his life would take. Then the Lord spoke to Jeremiah, *Before I formed you in your mother's womb I knew you.* (Jeremiah 1:5). God was reassuring Jeremiah of the relationship they had together before he was placed in his mother's womb.

Then there was King David, who wrote of the complex nature of man's beginnings. *I was not hidden from You while I was being woven together in my mother's womb. Your eyes saw my unformed body, and all my days were written in Your book and ordained for me, before any of them began.* (Psalm 139:15-16). God was present while he was in the womb. But it is even more incredible to know that God wrote the chapters of his life before he was placed on the Earth.

Another mystery unfolded in the life of a man named Manoah. An angel of the Lord appeared to him and his wife and told them God was ready to give them a son; a special son. They named the son Samson, and today his name is still associated with his incredible strength. This visit was to prepare Samson for the assignment he was predestined to do.

These incidents prove that man existed before the womb. Man's assignment and the purpose for which he was born, were carved out by God before he was placed on the Earth. *God has chosen us in Him before the foundation of the world, that we should be holy and without blame before Him in love. Having predestined us to be adopted by Jesus Christ, unto Himself.* (Ephesians 1:4-5).

To think that we existed before God laid down the first lump of clay He used to form the Earth, causes swells of joy in our hearts. Life can no longer call the shots or hold man back when he knows his destiny was spoken into existence long before he arrived on Earth. Destiny comes from a source beyond human capacity. Destiny is from God and is locked into the soul of man. The will of man and his reverence for God unlock his destiny, while his emotions drive him to fulfill his purpose.

It is not unusual for groups of people to deny the spirit world. In fact, it is common and easier for man to ignore and deny the things he cannot explain. The Sadducees were a religious group during the time of Jesus Christ who believed there was no resurrection, neither angels nor spirits. They went to Jesus to hear His perspective on marriage in the life after Earth.

Jesus replied, *When men shall rise from the dead, they neither marry, nor are given in marriage. Instead, they are like the angels who are in Heaven.* After this life on Earth is over, man returns to the state of being an angel.

In the Book of Ecclesiastes, King Solomon tells us that the spirit of man goes back to God, his Creator, when his business on Earth is complete. *Then shall the dust return to the Earth as it was, and the spirit shall return unto God who gave it.* (Ecclesiastes 12:7). If the spirit goes back to God, it means that the spirit first came from God. When man walks out of his earthly body, life has just begun, and that life will never end because man goes back to his original state of being a spirit. King Solomon, the wisest man to walk the face of the Earth, was given this knowledge. The Apostle Paul shared with the Church at Corinth how he entered the spirit realm and saw things he was not privileged to share. Daniel, who interpreted Nebuchadnezzar's dreams, and John the

Beloved, wrote similar experiences of their visions of the Heavens, capturing details of the end of time and life after death. However, true to the promise of God, Solomon received wisdom and knowledge that no other man on Earth has ever received—the spirit of man leaves his body in the grave and goes back to God.

Man comes from Heaven to the Earth as a spirit. This spirit is placed in the womb where it puts on flesh, and is made alive by the breath of God. This spiritual process of man being placed on the Earth was explained to Mary, the mother of Jesus. The conception of a child is the Presence of the Lord placing a spirit in the womb. The womb responds to the breath of God by bundling the spirit in a blanket of flesh.

Man is a spirit, and spirits are eternal. That is the reason we can be certain that when he leaves the Earth, man will live forever. Spirits never die; only things that are earthly have an expiration date. If it originated in the spirit realm, it will live forever.

This all-important process is loaded with purpose. Everyone chosen to grace the Earth is not just given life but given purpose—an assignment that must be accomplished. The assignment is to find truth. The burden of man is to find the path that leads him back to God. The greatest achievement of man is to master the unknown spiritual world while here on Earth. While it seems impossible to navigate the spiritual unknown, consider that every earthly success was previously unknown.

The answer to the origin of man must also coincide with the existence of God. If man came from God, there must be proof that God is real. In his conscious being, man knows there is God, but if no one has ever seen God, His existence may just be a myth. Earth is founded on the laws of evidence; therefore, the creator of the Heavens and the Earth must have left even a trace of evidence of His existence.

Man asks for the proof of God to be given to his sight, while God gives proof to his heart. The eyes are limited to what and how far they can see, but not the heart. The heart is an unlimited storehouse of the wealth and the power of knowledge. That which is placed in the limitless storehouse of the heart propels man through the critical circumstances of life. Every heart knows God, has experienced God, and has communicated with God. The Father has never left any heart without concrete evidence of Himself. God prefers to communicate with the heart of man because the heart is the seat of love, while the eyes are the wells of desire.

However, the eyes do have their proof. No one has ever seen the breath of man. We see the motions of our breath by the rise and fall of the chest, or we see molecules of frost mingled with the breath of man, but man's breath has never been seen. This is one of man's greatest mysteries because we use our eyes to detect breathing. We feel it, we hear it, we even smell it, and that gives us all the evidence our eyes need.

Man's breath is the breath of God, seen yet unseen. God is in every man, evident and present, as every man lives by God's breath. Man asks to see a physical form of God, but God is the breath, a Spirit without a physical form. That is why, to the physical eye, God is invisible. Just as man's breath is unseen yet visible, we see that everything consists of the invisible God. It must be the limitation of the physical eye, which also cannot see microscopic particles. The eyes cannot see that which is invisible. Man needs spiritual vision to look into heavenly matters.

The breath of man is evidence of the invisible God. When that breath leaves the body, the spirit of man goes back to

God, to whom it belongs and where it belongs, to live forever. Therefore, man will live forever because the spirit of man cannot die. That which is invisible cannot be killed, nor can it die. Man cannot kill that which cannot be seen.

Man knows he exists to write an eternal story because the eternal God lives in him. Each day as the sun rises, he paints on the canvas of time that which matters—I am here, I came from God, and my life will tell the story of God's grace. The man who has found himself has found the rarest treasure of the Earth. He writes the formula for success when he has solved the mystery of himself. Within that formula is the equation for eternal life—God is my father, purpose must not be delayed, and truth produces eternal confidence. He who has solved the mystery of man marches to an eternal beat, "I found myself."

THE WAR IN HEAVEN

Hidden in the twelfth chapter of the Book of Revelation, a great mystery unfolds which answers the questions of Earth, the existence of man, and the war that took place in Heaven. In this chapter, subtle references are given which reveal man fleeing from the war in Heaven to a place that God prepared. John, the disciple who leaned on Jesus' breast, was banished to a deserted island when he saw this vision.

Visions are dreams where the author is fully conscious and aware that a supernatural message is being given, a message which must be told. Just as in man's nightly dreams he moves from one scene to another, and from one geographical location to another, so we see shifts and movements of time and space in Biblical visions. Visions, like dreams, predict the future using references from the past and the present. However, visions become complicated when they use images that are not yet present in the Earth. The prophet Isaiah had a vision of the towers falling—Isaiah

30:25. The people of his day must have wondered greatly if the vision was true, or if Isaiah had gone off the deep end. More than 2,800 years later, the Twin Towers fell in New York, and the vision came to life.

The Apostle Paul wrote his letters from a series of visions he had with the Lord. In one of his visions, he discovered that those who were totally dedicated to Christ had no need for circumcision. This became known as a grievous and out-rageous lie. How could Paul denounce the law of God given to Moses? That was blasphemy! He explained to the people that circumcision in Christ had to become a spiritual act, where the sins of the heart were intentionally cut away, leaving a pure specimen of truth and love for the Lord. His explanation fell on deaf ears; in fact, it fell on ears that planned his death. The message of a vision can lie dormant until the time God chooses to reveal the depth of His heart.

The revelation John received on the Isle of Patmos hun-dreds of years ago, is now being unveiled in the true depth of its meaning. It shows man as the angels who went into hiding from the war in Heaven. Like an exciting motion pic-ture, the vision flashes back and forth, interwoven with sto-ries of the beginning, the present, and the future.

And there appeared a great wonder in Heaven: a woman clothed with the sun, and the moon under her feet, and upon her head a crown of twelve stars.

The woman represents humans of the Earth, clothed with the radiance and protection of God. Under her feet is the darkness of evil—symbolized by night or the moon. The sun is directly contrasted with the moon to show that even as God was present, so was evil. The crown of her head is Abraham's son, Israel the Nation, through whom God birthed the Christ child. The purpose of the crown is power. Israel has been given spiritual power from the hand of God to preserve the legitimacy and the Name of God. As a result, out of Israel came God's Church, which is God's spiritual Israel.

Similar to John's vision of the sun contrasting with the moon, was the event that was painted when Abram pitched his tent between Bethel and Hai. *And Abram moved to a mountain on the east of Bethel and pitched his tent, having Bethel on the west, and Hai on the east: and there he built an altar unto the Lord and called upon the Name of the Lord.* Bethel, being the House of God, is similar to being clothed with the sun; and Hai, being the alternate to God, is similar to the moon under her feet. The contrast is seen again when Moses visits with God on Mount Sinai. While Moses was at the top of the mountain having a face-to-face experience with God, the children of Israel were at the base of the mountain celebrating the golden calf of Sin-ai. The moon under her feet is a symbol of the sin-of-Ai; the sin of Sinai. Every place constructed for the true worship of God will always be met with an available counterfeit.

And the woman was with child, crying, travailing in birth, full of pain, as she waited for the moment of delivery.

The woman is crying out in pain, seeking to birth an answer to the disturbance in her life. It is important to remember that this vision is unfolding in Heaven. This part of the vision captures time before the beginning of the Earth, and sets the stage for the purpose of the creation of the Earth. God had a specific reason for creating the Earth; He created the Earth to give man time to reason out and fight for his eternal destiny. Earth is man's second opportunity to choose God and a source of relief from the turmoil that took place in Heaven. Empowered with the ability to think and reason, and given the time to weigh his decisions, Earth offers a host of comforts as man makes his choice. The anguish and painful cry of the woman is answered when God provides a place for her to hide, as seen further in the vision.

And another wonder appeared in Heaven. A great red dragon, having seven heads and ten horns, and seven crowns upon his heads. His tail drew the third part of the stars of heaven and cast them to the Earth.

While she is travailing in birth pains, another great mystery is taking place with a dragon who holds positions of great power. His power is so extensive that he wears seven crowns and rules over ten kingdoms in Heaven. This powerful red dragon has used his strong influence and significant rule to gather a third of the angels of Heaven, but they are cast out into the Earth.

Then the dragon stood before the woman who was ready to be delivered, so he would devour her child as soon as it was born. The woman brought forth a man child, who was to rule all nations with a rod of iron: and her child was caught up unto God, and to His throne.

The text is interwoven with glimpses of time before the beginning, glimpses of activities on the Earth, and glimpses of the end of time. John's vision, which is taking place in the heavenly realms, reveals that every activity on the Earth is first carried out in the Heavens.

Now, the dragon turns his attention away from the war to the woman who is ready to birth the answer to her woes. The relationship between the dragon and the woman is intertwined even though it is not clearly stated in the vision. The woman in pain is an extreme threat to the dragon. She is such a threat that he would turn away from the war to focus on the answer she is producing. The dragon understands the spiritual concept that answers which are birthed in the season of pain, completely destroy the fortresses of evil.

The dragon knows that this child will be his demise. If he devours the child, he defeats the woman because the child is God's answer to the woman's cry. If he devours the child, all the strength and power of God in the child become his. He needs this power to win the war, because the war is layered with mysteries from the heart of God. The cry of pain, the child with the rod of iron, the crown on the woman's head, all these mysteries are war-traps to defeat the dragon, and he knows it. He knows that spiritual defeat is eternal torment which riddles the mind with the bullets of pain until the body is tortured. This was no game, and he could not afford to lose.

Additionally, he cannot destroy the woman because she is wrapped in the protection of the Sun, a protection more powerful and far greater than his power. Spiritual law is also enforceable. Spiritual law gives her the power to trample that which is under her feet. The pain she is experiencing may have distracted her from her true power, but this was war, he had to become strategic or lose everything. The dragon chooses his battle wisely by waiting to devour the newborn; waiting to destroy the answer to the salvation of man—the Christ Child.

Now, the Son of God was already begotten in Heaven. Therefore, this birth was not the birth of the *Only Begotten Son* in Heaven, but the coming of Christ to the Earth. Man on the Earth, crowned with the shining jewel of the chosen Nation of Israel, gives birth to the Christ child who will destroy the power of the dragon. But in the vision, the dragon is waiting to devour the child, to kill the child as soon as He is born. This portion of the spiritual vision was played out in the Earth when Jesus was born in Bethlehem of Judea. King

Herod issued a command that all children under the age of two years *were to be devoured*, to be killed: but Joseph took Mary and the young child and fled to Egypt.

And the woman fled into the wilderness, where she had a place prepared by God.

In the midst of the war, the woman is crying out with birth pains to bring to life the only one who can put an end to the evil power of the dragon. Afraid, she runs away from the war. Here is a mysterious spiritual twist in the story. The wilderness is the hiding place prepared for those who fled from the war. John describes the environment of the hiding place as a lonely wasteland, while the Book of Genesis gives us the name of the place. From the details in the Book of Genesis, we learn that the place prepared is called Heaven. Then it goes on to report that the Earth was also created. A new Heaven and the Earth were prepared for the unfinished business of the war of Heaven. But the war is not over. Even as the woman goes into hiding, the war continues.

And there was war in Heaven: Michael and his angels fought against the dragon, and the dragon and his angels fought, but prevailed not: neither was their place found anymore in Heaven. And the great dragon was cast out, that old serpent called the Devil, and Satan who deceives the whole world. He was cast out into the Earth, and his angels were cast out with him.

The casualties of the war in Heaven were not killed, they were booted out of their positions of hierarchy and power. Spirits do not die, so the punishment for the spirits that fought against God in Heaven will never be death, but eternal damnation. To win the war, Michael and his angels fought to remove Lucifer and his angels from their positions. The evil of war has now been brought into the Earth where those who fled into hiding will have to wield their sword of choice.

John, in his vision, has now distinguished three groups of God's created beings. The fearful woman who started out as the main character of the vision, then the loathsome dragon who continued to fight even after she fled from the war. The weapons the dragon is using in this war are so powerful that he is identified by the names of his weapons. Old serpent describes his craftiness. Devil indicates the level of evil to which he stoops. Satan means, he uses his power as an accuser so viciously it deceives the whole world. Also, we know from the vision, this is Lucifer, the Son of the Morning. Finally, Michael and his angels are introduced and, in an instant, become the heroes of the war. All of God's created beings who now reside in Heaven or in the Earth, were present for that event which took place before the beginning of time.

In the vision, John witnesses God's solution to the war. God separated His angels into three distinct groups. The dragon and his stars (another term for angels), Michael the hero and his angels, and the woman who gives birth to the Christ child. As a result, God prepares three distinct places for the three groups of angels—places of abode according to their spiritual status. The Book of Genesis tells us that at the beginning of time, God created the Heavens and the Earth. Since God lived in Heaven, this was the creation of a second Heaven. The wilderness is created to become an extension of Heaven which is a hiding place to bring relief to the fear of the Woman. This confirms that before the creation in the opening verses of the Bible, God had already created all his angelic beings. The word *beginning* has been poorly interpreted. Beginning means a timer has been set and built into the design of the new Heaven and the Earth.

Later chapters of the Book of Revelation give details of the timeline of these events when it tells us that the Lamb was slain before the foundation of the world. As we examine the playbook of God, Jesus was crucified in Heaven before the Earth was created—before the foundation of the Earth was established. (Revelation 13:8). The Lamb was slain to bring healing to the damage created by the war. Additionally, a third of the angels were rendered unholy by the war, and it was necessary to cleanse them with blood. The angels who needed to be cleansed from the impurity of not choosing to honor God in the face of extreme pressure, were not Michael's angels. They fought for God's honor. Lucifer's angels were cast out of the presence of God and out of Heaven; therefore, they had no need for cleansing. The group of angels who fled from the war, who were overwhelmed with fear, needed to be restored to love.

Since God's angels need no cleansing and Lucifer's angels have alienated themselves from anything that is pure, the sacrifice had to be for man. The sacrifice of the Lamb took place first in Heaven, where it restored the divine order of God. But the work was not finished. The sacrifice had to be brought down into the Earth where man was placed to make his eternal decision. The sacrifice could not remain only in Heaven or those who fled would not be cleansed. God had to prove His heart of love to those who did not fight for His honor, by repeating the cruel sacrifice of His son on the Earth. The slaying of Jesus Christ in Heaven was after the war, but before the laying of the foundation of the Earth. The woman had gone into hiding before the war ended, and so she needed the sacrifice to be restored to God. But this was the moment of choice. Did she want to be restored to God, or was Lucifer's offer more appealing? The question of choice is answered when Adam and Eve chose to disobey

God in the garden of Eden. Now, there is an even greater need for the cleansing blood of Christ.

After accounting for all of God's created beings in the heavenly war, the vision speaks of the child the woman would give birth to—the savior of the war. The woman flees into the wilderness, and the child is caught up to God; then nothing more is said about the child. The Bible is a book of spiritual puzzles because, at the beginning of Jesus' ministry on Earth, He is led into the wilderness and offered the greatest sellout known to man. It is no coincidence that Jesus was led into the wilderness to have a face-off with Lucifer. The wilderness is the spiritual wasteland of loneliness and fear where men hide in order to survive. Jesus had to enter that place, not only because it is man's hiding place, but also because He is thereby legitimately confirmed as the man-child of the woman who fled.

Jesus being led into the wilderness, and the woman fleeing into the wilderness are glimpses into the mystery of Earth's connection to Heaven. In the wilderness, Jesus is tempted to make a bargain: He is enticed to give up who He is for what He wants. (Book of Matthew, Chapter 4). While in the wilderness, Lucifer offers three temptations to the savior of those who were contaminated by the war in Heaven. First, turn their stony hearts back to God. Second, test the protection of God; and the final test was an offer to restore all that God had lost during the war.

Sacrifices are most effective when the gift is treasured. In order for Jesus's death to be accepted as the way back to God, man had to believe in and trust the sacrifice. Before He was crucified, Jesus had to bond with man and convince him to love God with all his heart. Jesus had to soften man's stony heart. The hearts of those who fled into the wilderness were not fully persuaded towards God. God defines stony hearts or hard hearts as those who desperately want to obey God, but are pulled away against their own will. In the wilderness, Lucifer dared Jesus to make the stones into bread; to prove that He could change the stony heart of man. Jesus responded, "I will feed them with the word of God, and as they eat, their hearts will turn to their Father God again."

At the beginning of Revelation 12, the woman who fled into the wilderness was clothed with the protection of the Sun; the protection of God. Lucifer's second challenge was that Jesus test the strength of God's protection. Sounds as if Lucifer invented show-and-tell. He is always daring man to prove something. He told Jesus to become reckless and see if God would pull His protection. Jesus told Lucifer that He had no need to tempt God.

The third temptation in the wilderness gave Jesus the option to retrieve everything Adam had lost in the garden of Eden. Adam was given the key to establishing the Kingdom of God on the Earth, but it was stolen by Lucifer. Jesus was sent to take back the key to God's kingdom, but the process was through the torture of crucifixion. Lucifer offered the key, if Jesus would bow and salute him as god. Three temptations, all taking place in the wilderness, the place where man fled into hiding.

And I heard a loud voice saying in heaven, "Now is come salvation, strength, the kingdom of our God, and the power of His Christ; for the accuser of our brethren is cast down, which accused them before our God day and night. And they overcame him by the blood of the Lamb, and by the word of their testimony: and they loved not their lives unto death. Therefore, rejoice, you Heavens, and you that dwell in them, but woe to the inhabitants of the Earth and of the sea, for the Devil has come down to you, having great wrath, because he knows that he has but a short time."

Here, the vision tells us that man who inhabits the Earth are the brothers of the angels in Heaven. All of God's created beings are angels, but here, they are distinguished by their obedience to God—those who dwell in the Heavens, the inhabitants of the Earth, and the angels cast out for treachery. There are three distinct groups of angels.

Day and night, Satan stands before the Lord asking for the souls of those who did not join him in the heavenly war. The Heavens can rejoice because it has been purged from the evil, but the Earth is warned because it is about to experience fierce wrath mingled with evil. The process for defeating this woe is also given. The Earth must accept the blood of Christ, pass the test, and remain true to the Lord even unto death.

Lucifer and his gang have been kicked out of the Presence of God and from their position and power. They experienced spiritual death, which is separation from God. Physical death is only experienced in the Earth by man, and is simply the process of returning to eternity. The war, however, established a new Heaven, Earth, and the place created for Lucifer and his angels—the place called *Hell.* Man now has a choice to make, and that choice is not made by an intelligent answer, it is made by his actions. Will he choose to honor God while here on Earth, or will he choose the bondage offered by Lucifer?

In the latter parts of the Book of Revelation, a mighty angel with a rainbow above his head and a little book in his hand began to announce the end of time. He announced that *...the secrets of God are finished.* God has been sharing more and more of His secrets with those who have stopped to listen. These are the deep, end-time secrets of God's heart, mysteries which have been hidden from the foundation of the world. How do we answer the mysterious questions of the Heavens and of Earth? By proof to satisfy skeptics, but by faith to empower the righteous.

GOD AT WORK

A new era began in Heaven. The war gave rise to conflict that produced instant separation between the angels. Michael's sword defended God's honor against the betrayal of Lucifer, but so many of God's children were displaced, with no place of safety or belonging. The war in paradise sent God back to work, back to the drawing board, this time to create separate domains for His angels. *In the beginning*—of time—God went to work, and *God created the Heaven and the Earth.* (Genesis 1:1).

First, He created the second Heaven, a lonely wasteland which became the hideout for His children who did not fight for His honor. Wrapped into the design of His work were codes and mysteries, the most exciting of them being the concept called *time.* To activate time, He set a clock in the firmament which would rise each morning and go down every night. He surrounded the clock with smaller lights to flip the dial and reset time into years, and seasons, and days for an accurate countdown.

To confirm that creation of the second Heaven and the Earth is indeed a continuation, the Book of Genesis tells us that God had conversations with whom the text calls 'us'. The eighth chapter of the Book of Proverbs and the first chapter of the Book of John tell us that Christ was present with God for the creation of the second Heaven and the home of man called *Earth*.

When reading the Bible, it is easy to glaze over the mysteries and the concepts which do not carry suitable explanations. *In the beginning, God created the Heaven...* is a hard concept to follow because the details are limited to three short verses. It is easy to understand the creation of the Earth because it is followed by a continuous series of events throughout the entire Bible. On the other hand, the creation of Heaven seems to have ended abruptly. But glimpses of the wilderness of Heaven have been given in other places. A picture of the experience of the wilderness is painted as Moses leads the children of Israel to the promised land. They ate angels' food, water was given from the rock, and the Presence of God was a pillar of cloud by day, and a protective fire during the night. Before David became king of Israel, he roamed the wilderness, using it as a hideout from those who wanted to take his life. John the Baptist prepared Jesus' pulpit by preaching and baptizing in the wilderness. The second Heaven is indeed a holding place until the time that man is chosen to enter the Earth; a place that is full of the mercy and the grace of God.

God's first priority was to prepare a place for His children who were terrified by the war, so that their hearts could be at ease. Thus, God created an expansion of Heaven, a heavenly hiding place in the wilderness. *And God made the firmament, and divided the waters which were under the firmament from the waters which were above the firmament:*

and it was so. And God called the firmament Heaven. And the evening and the morning were the second day. (Genesis 1:7-8). This extension of Heaven in the midst of the waters was not airbrushed with wonder and excitement, it was just a holding place for the spirits who were afraid. The wilderness is designed to be a temporary experience. The spirits who lived in this second Heaven would be given their turn to enter into a more lavish home which would be decorated with the heart of God.

Then God moved on to the main dish, a more elaborate creation—the making of the Earth. As God created the Earth, He spent days carving, and decorating, and polishing the mountains, and rivers, and waters to make them shiny and appealing. He wove colors into the fixtures using light. The waters were charged with a replenishing force, and wherever there was water, there was life. Birds, animals, trees, flowers; the Earth was a breathtaking landscape of delight. Yet, coded into the design were layers of secrets that would keep unraveling, and unwinding, and exposing the infinite depth of God's mind.

We can now erase science's theory of Earth as a haphazard explosion of matter. Mindless, random activity is inconsistent with the perfection of order that has been coded into Earth's blueprint. The Earth is an intentional design of God for the purpose of choice. Just as a choice was presented to fight in the heavenly war, so Earth is about making a choice amidst its cultural pressures and wars. This dialogue changes the place we call Earth from a mere ball floating around in space, to a garden of relief, moments away from Heaven. Just as the lens of a camera is adjusted to bring a scene into focus, we can now appreciate the true perspective of life. Earth is not far away from God. Man can adjust his spiritual focus and communicate with God. Isaiah, the prophet, captured God making a tour of the Earth. *Behold, the Lord rides upon a swift cloud, and shall come into Egypt.* (Isaiah 19:1).

When the garden of Earth was ready, God took one spirit out of the wilderness, outfitted him with a tailor-made suit of clay, kissed him, and named him man. *Then the Lord God took dust from the ground and formed man and breathed the breath of life into man's nostrils. And the man became a living person.* (Genesis 2:7). Nothing else in the garden of Earth contained the breath of God. The kiss contains the mind and the power of God, along with the ability to reason and commune with God. Man, the spirit, was wrapped in a suit of clay and energized with the kiss, the authority to rule as God would.

This man, who was taken from the wilderness, was given the enormous task of fathering all the spirits who would be sent down from the wilderness of Heaven. He would succeed as a father by ruling the Earth and taking dominion over the darkness. The kiss of God ensured his success. The man would carry God's heartbeat and God's DNA and become creative as he ruled with the wisdom of his Father God. In this new home, man would enter into God's rest and forget the turmoil of the war of Heaven.

Now, it was time for God to rest. The work of cleaning up the debris of war was over. Michael and his angels would remain soldiers of the throne, man was created and placed on a timer, and Lucifer and the rogues were sentenced to eternal damnation. Now that the structures were created and the placements were done, the stage had to be set for choice. The man had not yet been purged from the sins of war, plus he had an enemy he could not see. Even though the odds seemed to be stacked against the man, God's hands were tied, because it was man's turn to create the rest of his story.

Ingeniously, God wove the secret of success into the heart of man, locked it into his will, and handed him the key of knowledge. Now, man had the choice of making his home a happy place by an act of his will, or making life miserable by inviting Lucifer to lunch. Knowing the outcome of the story of Earth, God weaved into the unraveling of time, secrets that would unfold and protect the heart of man. These details had to be protected, the mysteries of the Earth could not be revealed at the beginning, or the enemy of God would desecrate every plan.

All was done, and God rested.

TRUTH IS ETERNAL

How did Lucifer convince angels who lived in the presence of God to fight against God? What manipulative scheme did he weave into their souls that could possibly convince them they would win a war against God? Let's argue that in numbers, they believed they could match God's strength and overthrow the throne. How did they reason out fighting against the love of God? Whatever it was, it must have been soaked in a stiff gin that intoxicated the minds of those poor angels. It is easy to pity their state because man has sinned against God umpteen times and has enjoyed the luxury of God's love and forgiveness; but these poor angels lost everything on the first bad decision.

But how can there be pity? These must have been a real nasty brood of vipers because they have not given an inch since they were kicked out of Heaven. It is because of these demons that the occupants of the Earth have lived with wars and constant fighting—forever. These evil beasts wield their power, especially on innocent children, crippling them for the rest of their lives.

Man would perhaps win the fight against these beasts if he could see them. God should have given man eyes to see these spirits. The truth is, physical battles are fought by sight, but spiritual battles are won by faith. God knows that man, in his limitations, is no match for a spirit, especially the one who dared to overthrow His throne. Man must rid his mind of the weakness of *seeing is believing* because the battle cannot be won by the senses. Lucifer's best game is to manipulate the thoughts, and man is guaranteed to win if he resists in his mind.

Well, God should show His hand. If God showed His hand, it would not be choice; life would become a manipulation of man's heart to love God. But man is faced with making a choice amidst a fierce battle for his soul. In this battle, no one is spared from the devastation of the war, even in a state of ignorance. There lies the reason for choice. To ask God to intervene and show His hand is an easy escape from re-sponsibility. Earth belongs to man, not to the spirit world. Man must rise and protect his home and his heart from evil.

It does not help that God allowed innocence at birth in the absence of eternal truth. True, because the path to eter-nity demands loyalty. Soldiers who are dedicated to their army need not know the basis of the war. The generals study the battlefield, lay out strategies, and deploy soldiers to destroy even the traces of evil before laying stakes in the land. When the flag designating the overthrow is raised, the guards come in with a militant plan to protect that which has been taken. Those who love God must begin to fight for the Earth and for their brother. That is true love. Man needs to raise the flag of love and protect the Earth from evil. Evil cannot win against love.

But this is a fight for eternity, where there will be no end—forever. Why allow the peril of choice to determine the outcome of such an important destination? Those who love God have signed up to win the greatest battle of their lives. They are fighting to take back control of their families, and churches, and nations. In their eyes, it is not a matter of choice, it is a laser vision of focus on God. As a result, they refuse to be manipulated. They refuse to turn tails or run and hide—that show is over. Instead of asking 'why', they ask 'how'. They are now enlisted in an eternal battle, and they understand that this time it is do or die.

Make no mistake, the competition is stiff. Darkness throws wealth and affluence around during the fight to sway the minds of the gullible, piling it on so thickly, the whole world gloats in envy. Light withholds its treasures, and beckons to the faith of the fighter to simply trust that the absence of glitter by no means reflects the absence of God. Softly, God reassuringly whispers that His vaults cannot be compared to the temporary and meager rations of Hell.

This is not just any fight. This is the fight for eternal life, and this fight is rooted in love. I can hear God asking, "Do you love Me enough to give your life for Me?"

The evil one is not an inventor, he is an impostor: he is not a creator, he is a crafter. He must use as his base argument something man was offered by God. Carefully camouflaged in his offer will be the makings of pure lies. In the garden of Eden, Eve was a god. She lived as a god, but there was no one to affirm her. She had not proven her worth because there was nothing to prove; she had never been challenged. The gut instincts of Eve were absent because she had never been provoked; she had never been tested. Pity her untested state, for this was her introduction to the form of sin that would shape the rest of her life.

It is the weakness of man that leads him to be duped into trusting his eternal destination to Lucifer and his demons. Lucifer will use the same lie that set off the war in Heaven to entice man. He will offer value which man already has and teach man how to dishonor Christ. Even so, it is spiritually unnatural to choose darkness and man has to struggle with himself before choosing the lie.

Every man sent into the Earth is given two things, a number and an assignment. The number tells the number of days he will play in the stadium of life. The assignment states his position in the game and the accomplishments expected. The rules of the game and how to win are made up of values, discipline, and obedience to God. If man follows the rules, he celebrates life as an amazing player. God's game plan is a role call. God calls the role, man enters the stadium and plays until his time is up. The Earth will only exist as long as there are spirits to be sent into it. When the last spirits have exited Heaven and have finished their course on the Earth, the time-clock will stop, and life will return to its spiritual order.

No man will leave the Earth without the conscious knowledge of his Heavenly Father, but this knowledge is his to protect and to increase. The case of God's fairness or justice is irrelevant. God empowers man to choose because He will not manipulate His children. If God has to manipulate His children into loving Him, He is not worthy of being loved. God will not stoop to exploiting His precious children. On the contrary, Lucifer is not asking to be loved, he is dead set on having companions in the eternal flames of Hell; therefore, he stoops to the undignified, deceptive master scheme of lies.

Quite a compelling theory to answer the timeless questions of life. How do we know this is true? Truth is eternal, and man's spirit, which came from God, will never allow him to forget truth. Spirits know truth. Truth stirs up knowledge that has never been stoked and connects man's spirit instantly to the Spirit of God. In fact, after the truth is heard, it never leaves the heart. Truth is unforgettable. Truth is man's sword against the words of deception that seek to strip him of the robe his Father placed on him before he left His Presence. *If any man has an ear to hear, let him hear.* Hear what? The little nuggets that empower man to win this war—the kind, gentle words man hears deep inside his heart.

Before leaving His Presence to go into the Earth, God kissed each forehead. With His brows knitted and His loving hands holding each of His children close, He placed the bond of His eternal love in each heart. At the moment of exit from His Presence, God stamped onto each spirit the truth of His fellowship. He knows man would miss Him: miss the sweetness, the tenderness, the love. God knows that the missing bit would draw man to find His Presence in the woes of Earth.

Man has done everything to find love. He has spent fortunes, shed bitter tears, spent sleepless nights and days of perplexity searching for the joys of that special bond he had with his Father God. The never fading strength of that love is man's connection to God, as only love can bring him back to God. True love has no counterfeit, and the false version of love cannot last. The need for this intimacy cannot be quenched, nor can the joy of the connection man had with God be suppressed. No one can deny or escape the raging need for true love because it is the love that our Father burned inside the soul to draw man back to Him. On the strength of love, man is empowered to reject the lies, fight for truth, and make the choice to serve his heavenly Father for eternity.

PAGES OF TRUTH

The Bible does not reveal much about the character of Adam, the man who was given the charge to father the whole world. It gives a glimpse of his unique level of intelligence, and there is a hint of the genuine care he had for his wife. Beyond that, Adam's character or position within the angelic rank or in the garden seems relatively dull. Regarding the matter of his failure, there is no clear explanation why Adam went along with the plan to disobey God.

However, there is a case of suspicion as to why God allowed Lucifer to enter Adam's world. Lucifer was an archangel of Heaven, ruling over seven kingdoms and governing ten kings. This means the gift of the power of leadership was bestowed on this mighty angel. Why did God pit Lucifer against Adam? This spiritual boxing match between a giant and an amateur has the smell of purpose all over it. God must have thrown Adam into the ring as bait.

The man on whom the responsibility was laid to become father of the house failed, and he failed miserably. Using his creative genius, Adam devised a number of plans to cover his failure. When the dust settled, God came to visit–to sit and talk with Adam and Eve. This is a huge contrast of God's response to the sin of the war in Heaven. Lucifer and his gangsters sinned against God, and with one swift strike, they were banished from His grace forever. With Lucifer and his gang of deceivers on Adam's tail, God knew Adam was bound to sin.

Following the trend, and by sheer partnership with Lucifer, Adam should have been cast out of God's presence as well. There had to be a divine reason why Adam was spared. Adam became the bait that attracted God's love. The character of weakness in man is not repulsive to God; instead, man's weakness pulls on God's love. Every time man sins, God comes running to find and rescue him from evil. *God's love for the world is so great that He gave His Only Begotten Son,* (to absorb man's sins) *that whosoever believes in His Son should not perish, but have everlasting life.* (John 3:16).

It takes the wisdom of God to build a success story from a foundation of failure. God started the world by acknowledging the weakness of man, so no flesh would glory in His Presence. Man trips over himself when he finds success, and God runs to his rescue when he capsizes his boat. When man has been humbled by failure, God steps in and writes the correct formula for success. God has chosen to build His Kingdom on the weakness of those whose failure will become God's greatest love story.

Adam rewrote his story because he was more cunning than the serpent. He secured an eternal relationship with God for himself, for Eve, and for all his children. Adam's relationship with God was so strong that he birthed the character of forgiveness in God. Adam tugged at the heart strings of God and provided man with unlimited forgiveness as long as the Earth lasts. Out of Adam's failure came the gift of forgiveness, where God washes man's feet. *...that He might sanctify and cleanse it with the washing of water by the Word...* (Ephesians 5:26). *He poured water into a basin and began to wash the disciples' feet... If I do not wash your feet, you do not belong to Me.* (John 13:5, 8).

Adam knew God. Adam could accurately define God, he understood Him, he became a true son of God. Adam knew that God has great grace and kindness for those who struggle to find and serve Him. Yet, the greatest lesson learned from Father Adam is that God will never allow man to fight the battle with Lucifer all by himself—God will never leave. The act of sin can only be committed when man believes a lie, and God will extend mercy to those who are tricked into the slavery of sin. This means, man can move the heart of God to receive His love even when he is at his lowest. These were the stories Adam told his sons about his days in Eden. Their hearts must have yearned for that beauty and sweet fellowship with God—the Garden Days.

From these stories, God began a trail of information. These stories were not to exalt or defend Himself against Lucifer, nor to remind man of the days of Heaven, but to preserve the precious moments of His kindness to man on the Earth. Abel, Adam's son, wrote the standards for giving the best gifts to God. Enoch's life told the story of serving God with fierce loyalty that compels God to walk man back into Heaven without using the channel of death. Noah found grace in the eyes of the Lord and secured the covenant of God's mercy for man, even when God's anger becomes hot. Abraham's obedience promoted him to become the father of nations. God used Moses to begin writing these stories, and Moses named the writings, The Book of the Covenant.

These stories, preserved at the fireside chats of countless generations, became known as the 'Torah'. Like a great motion picture, the writings were stories of lives that were caught in the web of trouble, and through Divine intervention, these families found God's direction and were supernaturally saved.

But the power of Moses' writings lay in his face-to-face encounter with God. Hailed as the Prince of Egypt but a murderer on the run, Moses found a spot in the wilderness of the Mountain of Sinai where he spent time alone seeking the Presence of God. True to His word, God meets with those who forsake everything to find Him. The most captivating exchange between Moses and God was the finger of God writing on tablets of stone. During this encounter, God told Moses to build Him a tabernacle where He could meet with His people. This tabernacle was to be made exactly like the tabernacle in Heaven. For this assignment, Moses got a glimpse of Heaven. God wanted to have the same fellowship with man on Earth as it was in Heaven, so He gave Moses the blueprint to make the tabernacle like it is in Heaven. *...and there I will meet with the children of Israel, and The Tabernacle shall be sanctified by My glory.*

Through every line, the Bible shows that God captured a bit of His world and weaved it into the beautiful design called *Earth*. David became king of Israel generations after Moses. This king took the fort called Jerusalem and dedicated it to the honor of God. In his quest to write the most compelling life story of any king, David sat in the Presence of the Lord with his harp and composed psalms and songs that have outlasted history. In those moments of intimacy, David captured the vision of the coronation of Jesus Christ in Heaven. It was this coronation that infuriated Lucifer to commit treason against the Lord God and His anointed Son.

In the vision, David saw that this hatred would be carried into the Earth and that man would be beguiled into rejecting the Son of God. As he continued his meditation, King David began to weep and lament for God's Only Begotten Son. *You will not leave My soul in Hell nor suffer Your Holy One to see corruption.* (Psalm 16:10). David travailed in worship for the soul of Jesus Christ.

God placed another glimpse of Heaven in the Bible when He questioned Job, the rich man of the East. *Gird up your loins like a man, for I demand an answer. Where were you when I laid the foundations of the Earth? Declare it if you have understanding. Who measured it or stretched the line upon it? Where are the foundations fastened, or who laid the cornerstone when the Morning Stars sang together, and all the sons of God shouted for joy?* (Job 38:3-7).

Hidden in God's question is another celebration of His son, Jesus Christ, this time as the Chief Cornerstone. *Behold, I lay in Zion a chief cornerstone, elect, precious: and he that believes on Him shall not be ashamed...* (1 Peter 2:6). *Jesus Christ Himself being the chief cornerstone.* (Ephesians 2:20).

The Morning Stars were the angelic choir that hailed the ceremony with song while all of Heaven rejoiced. At this ceremony, all the sons of God were excitedly shouting with joy as Jesus was made the cornerstone on which the foundations of the Earth stand.

This conversation took place when Job was sick, almost to the point of death. In this most grueling bout with sickness, Job cried out, *God, why are You silent? I know You are going to bring me to death. When I look for good, evil comes: when I wait for light, there is darkness. My skin is black, and my bones are burned with heat.* (Job 30:23-30).

God's answer seems to make no sense, but listen to the voice of God as He brings the healing of worship to Job. "Before the Earth was made, I measured every line upon it: I fastened the foundations and laid the Cornerstone while the Morning Stars joined in the songs of worship."

This man's body was ravished by the darkness of death, and God is pouring spiritual life into his mortal body using the power of words. As God spoke, Job's body began to experience healing from his heavenly Father. It reminds me of my baby years, when I was sick and my mother would read stories to me. Her voice carried a precious healing power, and the stories took me into a world of fantasy where there was joy and peace. That peace flooded my soul, and I can still remember her soft hands as she touched me gently when she thought I had fallen asleep. God took Job into the healing power of worship where he experienced the purity of time before the beginning.

God continued to pour into Job's healing with questions. *Job, have you commanded the morning since the day you were born? ...do you know these things because you were alive when they were made or can you speak of them because the number of your days are eternal? ...do you know the ordinances of Heaven or can you set the dominion of Heaven on the Earth?"* (Job 38:12-41).

God would not pose a question without expecting an affirmative answer. "Job, are you waiting expectantly on Me to order divine healing to your body, and if I don't, then you complain that I am silent? Job, the morning is yours to command. Have you ever taken your God-given power into your own hands and demanded the day to come into alignment with your assignment and purpose? Do not wait for Me, command the morning; set the dominion of Heaven wherever you need miracles in the Earth. The foundations of the Earth are waiting for your command. Call My throne into agreement with your words. Job, speak!"

The ordinance of Heaven which Job needed was divine healing. God honored His vow not to rescue Job from the battle with sickness until the test was completed. But all the while, the power of healing was Job's to command. Job's sickness was prolonged because he did not know he could bring the power of healing from Heaven into his circumstances. So, God spoke and healed Job with words that became stories, that were written, that were preserved, that we might know.

Before Jesus' birth, the angel of the Lord was sent to a virgin named Mary. The angel said, *Behold, you shall conceive in your womb, and bring forth a son, and shall call His name Jesus.* (Matthew 1:21).

There is no doubt Mary had been praying that she would be chosen to bear the Christ child. Mary had to have been totally invested and fully engaged, making the angelic visit not a surprise but an answer to prayer.

The words of the angel were, *The Holy Ghost shall come upon you, and the power of the Highest shall overshadow you. Therefore, that Holy Thing which shall be born of you shall be called the Son of God.* (Luke 1:35).

Every Rabbi in Mary's day knew of the prophecy that a virgin would give birth to a son. Mary preserved her body and spoke faith into her mind to become the one chosen to bear God's son. However, her story of becoming the only virgin to give birth to a child overshadowed another powerful story that she has written. The angel of the Lord told Mary that the Spirit of God is present every time a child is conceived. For conception to take place, the Spirit of God overshadows the process, and He implants a spirit into the womb. Conception cannot take place unless that spirit is planted. The Presence of God is part of the conception of every person born on the face of the Earth, so every man is born as a child

Evil cannot penetrate conception, it has not been given that privilege; the process of placing a life in the womb is purely from God. Every pregnancy is God's gift of another spirit He has chosen to walk on the Earth. This is one of the amazing mysteries of life; man is a copy of God deposited on the Earth to execute the plan of God.

In reproduction, life is a sample of the original, containing tissues of the original. It is the same as carbon copies, which are imprinted, readable versions of that which existed. Reproduced life cannot contain genes that were not part of the conception—it is impossible. The genetic make-up of man is spirit, soul, and body. The spirit of man is a copy of God's Spirit because spirits were created by God and made in God's image. Man knows his father, God, because he is a duplicate of God's Spirit. As a carbon copy of the Spirit of God, he is the image of God, complete with the traits and power of God. Man is not an accident of conception. Every man is born with a purpose, on purpose.

It was with this fire of purpose that Saul of Tarsus burst onto the scene in the days of Ananias, the High Priest of Jerusalem. Burning with the fire of God, he went from city to city, breathing out threats and slaughter against the disciples who had turned their hearts to serve Jesus Christ. He was so fervent in the error of his heart, that the Lord had to pay him a personal visit.

"Saul, Saul, why do you persecute Me?"

And he said, "Who art thou, Lord?"

And the Lord said, "I am Jesus whom you persecute. It is hard for you to kick against the pricks." (Acts 9:1-5).

All these words and God-encounters were told and written, so man would be able to read on the pages of truth, the mind of the Lord. The most accurate record of life and history has been secured on the pages of the Bible. The earliest Biblical scrolls date back to 1200 BC, which makes the Bible one of the oldest books alive. Of its sixty-six books and approximately forty authors written hundreds of years apart, the themes and truths of its pages agree seamlessly. Despite its age, the Bible has not faded away or become obsolete. Instead, it has become a road map for events that unfold as time rolls on.

The Bible is spiritually, historically, and scientifically alive because every word of its stories paints the image of God. When man becomes genuinely curious about the existence of God, he turns to the only book he can fully trust. As he reads, he begins to hear God's voice and see God's heart. When he surrenders, he begins the journey of knowing God. When digging into the treasure of God's word becomes a time of intimate priority, he begins to find guidance, then comfort, and healing with wisdom. God did not leave His children without evidence; He is found in His word.

CHAPTER

8

ETERNAL INVESTMENTS

T he Bible gives us snippets of eternity with lots of details left to our wonderfully wild imagination–streets of gold, gates of pearl, te river of life. These all have a sort of celestial life to them which cannot be fully captured by the imagination, so the writer uses words to paint the picture. When the Bible speaks of eternity, it also tells us to avoid a black hole called *Hell*. It describes Hell as an ever-burning lake of fire, like a volcanic lava of hot, scorching sulfur. The Bible is also clear on the selected candidates for these two destinations–Lucifer and his squad of rascals to the lake of fire and God and His children to the streets of gold. However, the prevailing word is that there is no such place as Hell. While there is a ready acceptance of Heaven, there is also a clear contradiction on the topic of Hell.

All these discussions make it necessary to ask, "What does the heart of evil know that it relentlessly bombards man to reject the teachings of the Bible and write a different story?"

We can prove that the Bible is God's gift to man because it starts from the very beginning of time and accurately points man to the end. Proof that Hell exists and is set for eternal doom, is that it works overtime to discredit God and the Bible. If the Bible was just another fairy tale without truth or power, there would be no need to disprove its theory. However, because the Bible opens man's heart to the pathway of everlasting life, evil teaches man to push the truth away.

The truth that Hell is real will not go away, despite the many religions or stories that have labeled Hell a myth. The Bible tells us that man will live in eternal bliss with God while Lucifer and his demons will be roasting in the fires of Hell. Part of the reason evil is so livid about the Bible is that it offers man the free gift of forgiveness. Man sinned against God and received forgiveness; but they sinned against God, and there is no chance in Hell they will ever escape eternal torture.

And the devil that deceived them was cast into the lake of fire and brimstone, where the beast and the false prophet are, and shall be tormented day and night forever and ever. (Revelation 20:10). They sinned once and were not forgiven; man sins over and over again, and God is plentifully gracious.

That, however, is not the entire story. There is a stronger reason why Lucifer is nauseated with jealousy and destructive hatred for man. Lucifer knows that God has designated man to be ruler of the eternal world to come. Lucifer's thirst for power caused him to be cast down from the position of *Son of the Morning* in Heaven to the lowest Hell. His vicious overdrive to seduce men out of their eternal inheritance comes out of the venom of his own failure. He knows that men who make wise spiritual investments in the Earth will be the rulers and governors of kingdoms in the eternal hereafter.

God has not placed angels in charge of the world to come. But one in a certain place testified, saying, "What is man, that You are mindful of him, or the son of man that You visit him? You made him a little lower than the angels; You crowned him with glory and honor and set him over the works of Your hands." (Hebrews 2:5-7).

In the world to come, the eternal forever, the generals of this earthly war will rule over all of God's created beings. This war is an eternal investment, especially for those who will be crowned with glory to rule forever.

Jesus described the hereafter as a ruler who hired laborers for his business. On pay-day, he gave each laborer the wages promised. However, some who were hired murmured against the ruler because their hearts were evil.

Is it not lawful for me to do what I will with my own? Is your eye evil because I am good? So, the last shall be first, and the first last, for many are called, but few are chosen. (Matthew 20:15-16).

When the ruler rewarded good and hard labor, the evil came up with all kinds of criticism. Jesus showed that there are eternal decisions about who will be rewarded, how they will be rewarded, and how much they will be rewarded. There will also be decisions to elevate those who, by typical standards, deserve to be at the bottom of the pile.

Lucifer has one advantage over man: he knows how to feed man's weakness. Weakness is sin in its most elevated form, and it robs man of his eternal investments. Weakness aborts fellowship with God in exchange for a taste of the forbidden. The spirits of darkness satisfy weaknesses, but God gives man His strength to overcome that which destroys the soul. Life does get stubborn, sometimes with troubles stacked on top of each other, but trouble is the door to purpose. Lodged in the core of every battle is an eternal treasure that can be unearthed with the proper wisdom and knowledge.

When life tangles man in the bondage of destructive habits, the way out is to follow the principles of the Passover given by God to Moses. Passover is a spiritual ritual that breaks up and dissolves bondage, especially the bondage of witchcraft, and frees the soul and conscience completely. Bondage seems to have a generational twist to its hold, as many of the weaknesses can also be seen in parents and grandparents. The four-day Passover ritual God gave to Moses, was used to destroy 430 years of generational bondage and witchcraft. Nothing is impossible when man follows the teachings of God.

Another eternal investment is the heart cry of deeper repentance, where man enters into a place of solitude and seeks to be right with God. This soul-searching repentance takes back the permission man handed over to evil—the permission to lock him into the dungeon of weakness. Old memories loaded with guilt that seek to choke out the ability to be grounded are stuffed into the barrel of repentance and rolled down the hill of forgetfulness when man sits in the Presence of God with tears of sorrow.

To change the patterns of the past and write new stories, man invests in memorizing the Word of God. Memorizing scripture overwrites the negative words that are lodged in the subconscious. The spirits of evil point a laser target of defeat at individuals. They select the target at conception and follow that individual for a lifetime. At birth, they create a mess of confusion, and while the parents are busy sorting through the chaos, they steal precious emotional and mental stability from the child. The child will spend a lifetime searching for the stolen, missing link. Children who are robbed chase their tails trying to find the answers, even by indulging in destructive behaviors. If children are not introduced to their heavenly Father and the comforts of His word, the chase to become whole is a misguided hodge-podge of trial and error. Rewriting the words lodged in the subconscious—broken, loser, unwanted, misfit, de-pressed—takes the discipline of sipping on the Word of God until it is lodged in the memory.

Fasting is another spiritual principle which yields eter-nal results. Brokenness is a mental drain that steals the strength of discipline, but fasting restores self-control and provides the tools to mend the heart. First, fasting brings the soul face-to-face with the assaults and bullets of irre-sistible temptations. Next, prayer during fasting weaves a layer of protection over the soul against the attack, making the mind mentally alert and emotionally strong to resist the offers. Just as the body becomes weak without food, so the mind becomes wasted without fasting. Man draws the line in the sand, sets boundaries, and protects his eternal rewards in times of fasting.

Prayer is the live-wire connection with God, where man legally represents himself in the heavenly realm. When a case is filed in the courts of Earth, the party who does not show up loses the case. Man has lost his heavenly case over and over by being a no-show in the heavenly court of prayer. The Holy Spirit teaches man how to pray when he turns off the noise of the world and tunes in to God. All that is needed for the hard-wired connection is personal time with God and a true heart.

Perhaps the most significant eternal investment is the completion of man's God-given assignment. Imagine stand-ing before the Lord of Heaven and handing Him a treasure so unique, it makes every onlooker jealous. Every man knows he was born to do something unique and that is the gift he will hand to the Lord of Glory on his arrival in Heaven. That special assignment is buried in his soul. Every man knows his assignment because the thoughts never leave the mind. Life may squelch it with tons of pressure, but amid life's greatest problems, it finds its way to the forefront of the mind.

Paul wrote to the Philippians. *Let this mind be in you, which was also in Christ Jesus, who, being in the form of God, thought it not robbery to be equal with God, but made Himself of no reputation, took upon Him the form of a servant, and was made in the likeness of men. And being found in fashion as a man, He humbled Himself, and became obedient unto death, even the death of the cross. Wherefore, God also has highly exalted Him, and given Him a Name which is above every name: that at the Name of Jesus every knee should bow, of things in Heaven, and things in Earth, and things under the Earth: and that every tongue should confess that Jesus Christ is Lord, to the glory of God the Father.*

Paul is saying, when the tests of life become brutal, resist the temptation to let the mind indulge in the pain. Instead, choose to become Christ-like while the test runs its course. Taking on the form of Christ, which is the character of Christ, means all things of the Heavens and of the Earth will bow. Why? The values and principles of the mind have become equal to God. In this conscious state of equality with God, man is invited to test and to prove how to make perfect investments. Eternal investments are birthed out of spiritual rituals that secure man to God for eternity. The investment tools used to trade in the heavenly market are character, principles, habits, and values. The sum of these personal internal investments forms the link to the chosen eternal destination.

And do not be conformed to this world, but be transformed by the renewing of your mind, that you may prove what is that good, and acceptable, and perfect will of God. (Romans 12:2).

Man who is equal to God does not question the legitimacy, existence, or identity of God. He becomes settled and at peace, and not just by faith. That which was purely faith has morphed into proof because God's promises came to life. God now connects with the spirit of man on an intimate level, and the man begins to live in the experience of God, sharing God's heart, and God's thoughts—becoming one with God.

In God, as God pours treasures into his soul, he begins to serve a greater purpose than self; greater than that which is seen with the physical eye. God becomes his success story as he becomes an extension of that which is truly God. He begins to create like God, becoming a replica. He is not God. Instead, he becomes a son of God because all that he is, is God—the image, the heart, the light, the power, the love. The man, by his investment, is restored to that which is intended for those who bear the image of the heavenly. The earthly has captured the eternal and transformed it into infinity, crowned with glory and honor to rule forever.

CHAPTER

9

HEAVEN BROUGHT TO EARTH

History shows that there have been four great rulers who have shifted the direction of Heaven and Earth. They have been incomparable in their conquest and have set the standards of leadership so high, we know that neither the Heavens nor the Earth can or ever will produce their equal. Their conquests prove that all were leaders in the presence of God before the beginning of time. Jesus explained the timeline when He said, *...and now, O Father, glorify Me with Your own Self, with the glory which I had with You before the world began.* (John 17:5).

The greatest conqueror of all time is Jesus Christ of Nazareth, the Son of God. Some will argue that he possessed supernatural powers given His miracles and doctrine which He used to change the Earth. He gave the poor and outcast the means to tap into His power and rise to greatness. His teachings elevated women from being prostitutes or mere housewives to their rightful place in society. He outlawed crucifixion, not by the sword but by love. He protects little children against predators. He left the miraculous power of healing in the Earth—the work of Jesus Christ is too much to tell. Yet one thing stands out above all He ever did. By ascending into Heaven, He opened up a physical pathway for man to enter into the presence of His Father, God. This pathway was also for God to always be present with man.

It is hard to decide the order of greatness for the other three legends. All that can be said is that their impact has been tangibly noted in Heaven and on the Earth. The most daring of them all is Lucifer, who was the Son of the Morning in Heaven. His heavenly title indicates he rode on the wings of each new detail, designing and orchestrating plans that pleased God. He was chosen as a son—not the *Only Begotten*, but a son nonetheless. Since his fall from grace, his name and his character have been tied to every lying, hateful, and evil deed, including hell and death. Yet, this creature has managed to lie his way into the hearts of men, convincing them that the way to Hell is the most admirable way to live. He manages the kingdom of darkness so well that he is able to draw kings, rulers, and even the most intellectually savvy into faithfully serving him.

Another great leader that must be admired, yet he has given up the spotlight in honor of Almighty God, is Michael the archangel. He is given military power, spiritual ammunition, and no doubt a great sword; but his power has only been used to protect the glory of God. This angel rounded up a troop and defeated Lucifer in the realms of the Heavens. Throughout the Bible, Michael is a defender of God, protecting God's interests: showing up in battle after battle, fighting for God's honor. In his fights, he has never lost a battle, signifying this angel is a giant of a warrior. It seems reasonable to think that if God gave the signal, Michael and his angels would completely wipe Lucifer and the gang of deceivers out of existence.

The last of the four is a man whose name has transcended time to become the father of many nations and the father of the Church. The Apostle Paul, writing to the Roman Church of his day, asked this most important question. *What can we say that Abraham, our father, has found?* Abraham found that which most men have never dreamed of. He found the meaning for which he was placed on the Earth—to become the archangel of the Nation of Israel and of nations who would return to God.

Examining the conquest of these leaders, it becomes evident that Christ was truly the son of God, because none compares to Christ. Archangels, or chief angels, are rulers over hosts of angels. Christ's assignment was not to rule angels but to become the heir of God and to bring the Spirit of God into the Earth. Michael was given an army, Lucifer has an army, and Abraham was chosen to lead the angelic army of Earth. These leaders were specifically chosen, and because their assignments were spiritual, it means their tasks were handed to them before the foundation of the world was laid. *Blessed be the God and Father of our Lord Jesus Christ, who has blessed us with all spiritual blessings in heavenly places in Christ. Just as He has chosen us in Him before the foundation of the world.* (Ephesians 1:4).

The puzzle has now been pieced together, allowing us to see the grand scheme of God Almighty. Whenever God is going to shift the Earth, He always handpicks a leader and sets him over the work. God is predictable because He governs Himself by His rules, and His rules never change. Therefore, when God knocks at the door, it means the call came yesterday, today, and forever—before you were born, while on the

Earth, and for eternity. *Jesus Christ, the same yesterday, and today, and forever.* (Hebrews 13:8).

The outcome of God's work is certain; He does not govern by trial and error. *I, the Lord, have called you in righteousness, and I will hold your hand, and will keep you, and give you to be a covenant for the people. (Isaiah 42:6).*

Whatever He has assigned the individual to conquer will never be a statistical probability, or a wait and see; neither will God give an assignment that cannot be attained. *Before I formed you in the belly, I knew you; before you came out of the womb, I sanctified you and I ordained you as a prophet to the nations.* (Jeremiah 1:5).

The work of the archangel, gathering nations to God, was committed to Father Abraham yesterday (before the beginning of time), today (while he lived on Earth), and forever (a never-ending assignment). This man was selected to change the world—to birth kings, and rulers, and the Savior of the World.

We have our first record of a man called Abram in the Book of Genesis receiving instructions from God. *Get out of your country, away from your relatives and your father's house, and journey to a land that I will show you, and I will make of you a great nation.* (Genesis 12:1-2).

No mention is made of his previous interaction or his knowledge of God, so it leaves us asking the same question as Paul. "How did Abram make his connection with God? Was there something special about Abram, or is this type of encounter typical for those who seek to find God?"

Abram lived in Mesopotamia, which is called the cradle of civilization, generations closer to the beginning of time. That is uniquely important because God's assignment for this man is to birth and father nations. How does one man father a nation, or many nations? There must have been a secret to Abram, the man himself, and his relationship with God, because he captured the full picture of life, framed the vision, and built his world within the frame. Abram understood the meaning of the Earth in relation to the purpose of his life. That was how he earned the privilege of becoming the father of many nations.

Abram bore two sons, or two nations. These men were radically committed to his legacy and did not allow their father's faith to die. From these sons were spun every major religion that exists in the Earth today, thereby allowing the life of their father to influence the soul of every nation on the planet. Religion as we know it, has been copied from the pages of Abram's interaction and worship of God. There is no doubt that copies of his faith have been falsified, corrupted, misinterpreted, and some have become just downright rebellious expressions of the original. The point is, Abram's connection to the God he found is still the footprint of religion as we know it.

The how and why still linger. The more we delve into this mystery, the wider the sum of questions, and the fewer solutions we have to make the equation. But it is reasonable to argue that Abram must have been tempted to mingle his faith in God with the religions that surrounded him. He could have been like the group of outlaws who built the Tower of Babel in search of God. Those were the days when men studied the stars to gain spiritual powers; he could have become a star-reader to meddle with times and seasons. The ritual of sacrificing children as an offering to a god was also a common practice, and offerings to gods would have been an abomination to Abram's God.

What did Abram know that kept him faithful to a God he had never seen, especially when his culture believed in gods they could touch and handle? After all, Abram found the God of the spirit world; he must have been searching, he had to have been meddling in the spirit. He must have been tempted to mingle his obedience to God with the indulgences and rituals of his culture. No one gets to this God-level without enormous, incalculable temptations.

Was it a simple thought? Did he hear a voice, or was it a constant conversation in his mind to which he began to pay attention? Whatever it was, Abram built his belief around it and eventually invested his life into becoming a friend of this God he found. As we know, through this relationship, he inherited the right to father the generations that followed him.

When that same visitation came to Einstein, he calculated and plotted numbers to offer the world something it never had. When it was Caesar's turn, he flexed his political muscle and expanded the Roman Empire. It is easy to see that almost every man is somehow granted a visitation with the powerful God where his mind is opened to amazing possibilities of fame, wealth, and power. Abram did not establish governments or control territories, nor did he build cities and carve his name in them. He could also have constructed monuments that would tell of his great find; but instead, Abram preserved his faith by becoming a friend of God. Now his title reads, Father of Faith, Father of Righteousness, Father of the Church, and Father of Many Nations.

Every man is introduced to God, as he was, but to meddle in the heart and the plans of God is for those who do not become distracted in their pursuit. Abram was absorbed by an overwhelming desire to have a son. Ironically, God's plan for his life meant he had to have a child, so his obsession was indirectly God-centered. However, it was after he learned to control his desire, that he got the joy of having a son through the womb of his bride. The moment he became consumed by his relationship with God, the mantle of fatherhood was released to him.

To prove the depth of his commitment, God asked Abram to offer a sacrifice. The purpose of the sacrifice was to activate a covenant, and the terms of the covenant would give God permission to write the details of the rest of Abram's life. A covenant is an unbreakable promise, and in this covenant, God promised to give Abram the world as his inheritance. Since God initiated the promise, the burden of bringing it to pass was on God. *The promise that he should be the heir of the world, was not to Abraham or his descendant through the law but through the righteousness of faith.* (Romans 4:13).

Sacrifices are offered on two levels. First is the quality of the gift, and the second is the depth of the investment. This was the test that transformed Abram from an ordinary man to chief leader of the angels being sent into the Earth. Abram brought the Kingdom of Heaven to Earth and resumed his position as the leader of the angels who did not fight in Heaven. The role he had in Heaven was handed to him when he discovered who he was on the Earth. He fulfilled the word, *Your Kingdom come, Your will be done on Earth as it is in Heaven.* (Matthew 6:10). Abram discovered the secrets of Heaven and activated them in his earthly life.

The eternal God is a God of fellowship and divine order. God told Abram to obey His voice: keep His charge, commandments, statutes, and laws. God's voice is that which is downloaded to the senses. It gives clear instructions, but the senses will argue with the *why* or *why not*, the *if* or *if not*, the *should* or the *should not*. The soul must ignore the senses because fellowship with God demands total obedience.

The charge meant guarding the function—securing the details which were committed to him. Abram had to preserve and watch over the integrity of that which he was told to do. He kept it by performing ceremonial functions as a priest would, guarding the charge by imposing the lessons of God on his sons. He became a priest of that which was committed to him, and he dutifully carried out the order by guarding the charge of God.

The commandments are the codes of wisdom, the order and duties given by God to preserve the property. These were offerings he was mandated to give back to God. Obedience to the commandments would make him and his sons wise towards God. In keeping the commandments, they brought the lifestyle of God into the Earth. It was his duty to see that God was well pleased with that which was required of him. The commandments then became a prescribed tradition; that is, written and obligated.

The statutes are the customs he had to follow. These traditions were written into the culture of the nation. It is amazingly beautiful to watch the dance of Abram's sons. No other nation on Earth dances the way they do. Perhaps Abram had no rhythm, but because part of the culture was worship, he had to find a way to move. Abram used the statutes of God to create a unique culture.

Ordinances are permanent rituals unto Yahweh to be observed forever throughout all of Abram's generations. Most of the ordinances handed down through Abram are performed today in the synagogue. The anointing of the priests, the lighting of the candles, and the presentation of the Bread of His Presence, are rituals that honor the holiness of God. Though many of these ordinances came at the time of Moses, Abram has to be credited with preserving the integrity of the covenant.

The laws were legal directions to govern the nation. They were the instructions, codes, rulings, and teachings to make the nation great. For a more perfect understanding, the commandments are the highest standards of the law. For example, the commandment *Thou shalt not kill* was so prominent, it was known to all. Beyond the ten great commandments, the general laws were studied and kept alive by the scribes and lawyers.

The reason God visits with man is to unlock his potential. The voice of God—His charge, commandments, statutes, ordinances, and laws—are the same laws by which Heaven is governed. God poured His voice into Abram to bring Heaven to Earth. The voice of God is the key which man uses to unlock the impossible. *...and I will give you the keys of the kingdom of Heaven.* (Matthew 16:19). The voice of God awakens the full potential of those who enter the Presence of God frequently.

It is said that light is the process of passing photons or rays of electronic magnets at high frequencies through an object. Abram opened up his mind to become a channel which God could frequently pass through. Man is a magnet for God's Presence. Frequently adding the voice of God to the object of the mind, results in light. It is the body's chemical reflection of the Almighty God, who is the spiritual source of light.

The commandment is a lamp, and the law is light. (Proverbs 6:23).

Your word is a lamp unto my feet, and a light unto my path. (Psalm 119:105).

The entrance of Your words gives light; it gives understanding to the simple. (Psalm 119:30).

Jesus said, "I am the light of the world. He that follows Me shall not walk in darkness, but shall have the light of life. I

AM come a light into the world, that whosoever believes on Me should not live in darkness." (John 8:12).

For You will light my candle. The Lord my God will enlighten my darkness. (Psalm 18:28).

Then I saw that wisdom excels against folly (mental brokenness)*, as light excels darkness. (Ecclesiastes 2:13).*

The people who walked in darkness have seen a great light. They that dwell in the land of the shadow of death, upon them has the light shined. (Isaiah 9:2).

The Lord shall be to you an everlasting light, and your God shall be your glory. (Isaiah 60:19).

When man allows the current of God's Presence to flow through his flesh—frequently, very frequently, and especially at high frequencies—he experiences the glow of God. God's glory.

GOD INTERRUPTS TIME

A bram must have been as solid as steel in his commitment to God. His obedience made God walk forward in time to bring the treasures of the future into Abram's present. To prove that His ordinances never change, God arranged a physical meeting between Abram and Jesus, even though Abram lived fifty-six generations before Jesus Christ was born. This meeting legitimized Abram's spiritual and eternal position. Jesus confirmed it in the book of John about two thousand years after the meeting when he said, *Truly I tell you, before Abraham was, I Am.* (John 8:58).

To bring the culture of Heaven into the Earth, God needed a sacrifice, and every spiritual sacrifice must be offered with blood. Even further, to satisfy the holy requirements of God, sacrifices that change the Earth must be offered with the blood of Jesus Christ. God declares, *I am God, I change not;* but Christ was not scheduled to be born in the Earth until years after Abram. Therefore, God had to circumvent His own plans and bring Abram face-to-face with Jesus so that His Word would remain true.

To pull his assignment out of the spirit realm and execute it in the Earth, Abram needed to enter into a heavenly covenant with God. To enter into a heavenly covenant, he had to have had a heavenly experience. To enter the Heavens the Bible says, man must be born again. *Except a man is born again, he cannot enter into the power of the Kingdom of Heaven.* (John 3:5). Man in the Earth is flesh, and flesh cannot enter into the spirit realm. To be born again means that the Holy Spirit infuses man with the Spirit of God. When the man receives that conversion in his spirit, he is equipped to do business in the Heavens. He is now born of the Spirit, and being transformed into the purity and power of the Spirit, he can do the things that spirits do–like entering Heaven.

Born again only comes through Jesus Christ. Jesus is the door man must pass through to enter Heaven. Since God never changes His laws, He sent Jesus Christ as a high priest named Melchizedek to serve Abram bread and wine. Coming from the hands of Christ, the bread and wine became the body and blood of Christ–the blood that was shed before the foundation of the world. Christ, as a high priest, met Abram and sanctified him for the task he was born to do. This meeting of Abram and Christ solidified the heavenly covenant and the born-again experience Abram needed to become the father of nations. Jesus Christ issued the spiritual license Abram needed to pull his assignment from Heaven into the Earth.

God reworked time and favor to secure Abram's future. Once the blood covenant was satisfied, God became a father to Abram and changed his name to Abraham, This covenant activated the rights and privileges of sonship with his Father, God. Being fathered by God, he possessed the grace to pass on the father-heart of God to nations. As a son of God, he also inherited God's legacy, which is the Spirit of Holiness, and passed it on. Such an awesome responsibility to carry the legacy of Heaven into the Earth.

Leader of many angels in Heaven–archangel, to father of many nations on Earth–he found greatness. Abraham found himself through a holy covenant.

Look for a moment at the generals who were possible candidates for this rank and assignment. Adam–he gave up the call when he failed to exercise authority over his wife. Cain was asked to make the investment, but something was bleeding in his heart, which destroyed his credibility to become a son. Able was murdered; therefore, he was made to continue in name only. Noah found grace in the eyes of the Lord, but after his great accomplishment, he suffered a huge setback, not capturing the vision of a greater assignment on the horizon.

God was diligently searching for that one man on whom He could lay His mantle of fatherhood. *Father* is the highest and greatest title a man can ever hold. Abraham did not need any great feats to enter into God's hall of fame. All he had to do was defeat the spirit of distraction to carry on the DNA of his Father God. This is the portion that is often overlooked; Abraham had to pass the test–not a test–but the test that was specifically designed to prove his loyalty and commitment to God.

The test is not a fluke that can be brushed aside. The test has built into its core every desire, dream, need, fantasy, and lack that was never imagined. When the test is presented, it assaults the senses with aromas that send the mind into a state of madness. As temptation wafts its ugly head, the body dances to a tune that makes the bones melt. Abraham had to turn off the music and crawl back to God to inherit the promise. Listen to the moment he tells his wife, "…the plan you hatched, the one to which I agreed, is now yours to fully execute as you please."

Abraham did not have another child when he gave Sarah permission to drive his son out of their home. Could that mean he had disconnected his senses from his desire in order to focus on God? How was he going to father nations when he had to abandon his own son–his only son? Fathering meant he had to ensure that his son followed him to the portals of Heaven. This sounds like the Father God abandoning His Son on the cross. This abandonment was part of the script to be written by Father Abraham. He had to trust the power of God the Father to never lose his son, and to never cause harm to that son who was inseparably connected to him.

What did Abraham, our father, find? Abraham found his heavenly identity while he was in the Earth. He found his place in God through Christ Jesus and secured the covenant of fatherhood, handing down the legacy to his sons. Abraham wrote the manifesto on nation-building, of man uniting to faithfully build communities that last. Though he never established an earthly government, this man passed on the spiritual gene of uniting and building culture to all those around him, and they all began to build nations; not just clans. All who touched Abraham's life became nation builders, and all who believed in Abraham became successful through their faith.

Besides the Nation of Israel, the Church of Jesus Christ is the greatest legacy of Father Abraham. Abraham wrote the bill of instructions for the Church to revolutionize the Earth century after century. Today, the Church leads the charge to open men's eyes to the activity of evil in the Earth and is the only entity that has the power to stop the forces of darkness. One of the reasons the Church can never die and Israel can never be conquered, is the blueprint of faithfulness branded and handed down by Father Abraham.

CHAPTER

11

HOLY FIRE

Jesus came to the Earth and laid His tracks in the footprints of Father Abraham, taking man beyond the unity of nation-building and religion into a one-on-one relationship with His Father God. Through Jesus Christ, man has been issued an invitation to enter Heaven and have audience with the only true God. Abraham is proof that man is ordinary until he accepts the invitation to visit with his Father God.

Abraham lived in a culture where it was customary to marry and have children who would become a mighty clan. The more children a man produced, the mightier, and greater, and richer he was. Abraham was a disgrace by the standards of the culture because his incredibly beautiful wife was barren. His life was a dance with shame. The man was cursed because, without children, he had no identity within the culture. This sent Abraham into a state of mental confusion; it could not be that everyone around him was prospering while he was the chosen outcast. This was the driving force that sent Abraham on the search for God. Abraham pulled on God until he surpassed the demands of the culture. Through God, Abraham reshaped the tone of the culture to this day.

Jesus explained the process of becoming great in the Earth to Nicodemus, the Jewish ruler. To become great in the Earth, man must be born again. Man becomes overly disappointed when he is stuck in the nothingness of life. Born again is an invitation from God to enter into the Heavens and return to Earth with supernatural power. This covenant through Jesus Christ is a sacred spiritual birth. To become great, and to release his heavenly assignment, Abraham had to have this encounter with Jesus Christ. This covenant with Jesus Christ is not negotiable because Jesus Christ is the door to Heaven. Taking it a step further, God has deposited all His powers into Christ, and all who become immersed in Christ become heirs of the treasure.

Marvel not that I say you must be born again. (John 3:7).

If any man thirsts, let him come to Me and drink, (drink of the Holy Spirit). (John 7:37).

The Spirit itself bears witness with our spirit, that we are the children of God, and if children, then heirs—heirs of God, and joint-heirs with Christ. (Romans 8:17).

Not only did Abraham enter into the blood covenant when he met with Melchizedek, he also became born again and sanctified through Jesus Christ. If Jesus got Nicodemus to understand the spiritual, born again birth, Heaven would touch Earth.

Man had to give up his heavenly, angelic attributes to be born into the Earth. That included his knowledge, abilities, and even his Heavenly features. Angels are spirits, but when they are sent into the Earth, these spirits are tucked away, hidden in a body which is full of limitations. The Earth is also riddled with laws that restrict the physical and mental power of the man. The law of gravity dictates that he needs wings to fly. The law of mass restricts his movement. The law of sight regulates his vision. The imbalance of hormones induces stress. None of these laws prevent angels, and Satan's crew remained angels when they were cast down to the Earth and began the war for the souls of men. Neither God's angels nor Lucifer's angels are subjected to the laws of Earth because they are not subjects of the Earth. For years, man has had this unfair advantage in winning the war against Satan and his temptations. The disadvantage ended when Jesus Christ explained the process of being born again to Nicodemus.

"Truly, truly, I say unto you, except a man be born of water and of the Spirit, he cannot enter into the kingdom of God." (John 3:3).

Man is flesh and angels are spirits: the man needs divine help or he will wear himself to death trying to defeat the woes of evil. Man wars against his brother to cure his woes because his vision is limited and he cannot see the vicious fallen angels manipulating his brother into committing evil. However, no matter how he wounds or kills his brother, he has never been able to cure the evil. He must turn his attention to the spirit world in order to win his battles because his defeat comes from the spirits he cannot see. This makes for a blind fight, as it is impossible to fight that which is invisible.

When born again takes place, man becomes endowed with the same power that resides in God. God's vision, strength, and knowledge—all he needs to win the war—are provided when he becomes born again. It also positions the man in a higher rank than angels; and not only that, but the man is able to command earthly change through his born again spirit. To be born of the Spirit means man becomes spirit. The man is restored to his status as an angel. *That which is born of flesh is flesh, and that which is born of spirit is spirit.* (John 3:6). The man is now a spirit, living on the Earth, full of the abilities of God, full of the knowledge of God—full of wisdom, and love, and vision.

No longer is the man limited to the laws that govern the Earth, and no longer does the man just wait for life to push and shove him beyond his control. He is not on par with the angels, but above par, able to defend his life through the power of God. When understood correctly, man uses his born again spirit to stop the destructive activities of Satan and the demons. The man has the power to restore his world and create the perfect life here on Earth.

When man says, "I am born again," he is saying he is a spirit and he understands the power of being a spirit. Born again means he can go into the Heavens, hear the heart of God, and return in the power of God to the Earth.

I Am the door; by Me, if any man enters in, he shall be saved, and shall go in and out, and find pasture. (John 10:9).

Born again means the man has a seat at the table in the courts of Heaven making executive decisions for life and eternity. Born again entitles him to command the impossible to be done. When Jesus told that to Nicodemus, the world turned on its hinges. No longer was man subject to the torments of evil: no longer did he need to be a prisoner held down against his will by darkness, or oppression, or desires, or the war in his mind. Born again means slavery is over.

As flesh and blood, man is a puppet for the angels who roam the earth. As a born-again, Spirit-filled, son of God, he takes on the nature of God and is empowered to command his world with the same authority as Jehovah God. Born of the Spirit means restored to that heavenly status, the purity of angels in the Presence of God. For those who are born again, God says, *I will pour out from My Spirit onto your flesh.* (Joel 2:28). Therefore, flesh is no longer limited to the law of flesh. Flesh now becomes activated by the Spirit of God. The man is now a son of God who resides on the battlefield of Earth, empowered to win the war against Satan and his demons.

Adam was the first earthly son of God and carrier of the spiritual DNA of God, which he would pass on to his sons, and their sons, and to the whole world. However, before Adam could pass it on to his first son, Lucifer came in disguise and adopted him. This adoption was made legal by the exchange and acceptance of an offer. Lucifer offered to make Adam into a god, and Adam surrendered his God-given power to Lucifer. Adam then became the foster son of this spirit whose DNA was as black as hell. Adam became a carrier of Lucifer's gene. Now, all of Adam's children inherit the spiritual genetics which write the code for sin and have a distaste for holiness.

God's eyes are roaming to and fro the Earth to find those whose hearts are diligent toward Him, those who will carry His Spirit without compromise. God is still searching for those who choose to become born of His Spirit and refuse to wander back into the filth of compromise to commit the unpardonable treason that the father of mutiny is so famous for. Jesus Christ opened the door for man to change his earthly status from mere mortal to Spirit-filled, born again, sanctified by holy fire, angelic beings in the Earth. This is the gift of God to the born again.

EDEN FOUND

Man is conditioned to believe that all things must exist and be sustained according to the reasoning of his finite mind. Therefore, ecause he was born, because he began, and because all things within his world can be traced to an origin, he believes everything inside or outside his world must be guided by the law of beginnings.

Only things that can be seen with the physical eye are controlled by the law of beginnings, which answers the questions of how, and where, and the concept of time. The Earth is a living womb which gives birth to men in an element called *time,* so men would war for their eternal souls. The only reason that time exists is that man would exercise his privilege of choice. Before the Earth, or before time, a world existed with which we are very familiar. In that world, there were no beginnings, nor does it have an end, because it is not regulated by the law of time. Only things which are connected to the physical make-up of man's world are subject to time.

God is not on a timer, God is not a man, God cannot be traced, God was not born, and God will not die. This becomes a hard concept for those who live by the science of proof. Proof takes evidence and manipulates it until it can be mastered, and the same should be true about God. The problem is that man who desires to reduce God to science, cannot find Him. It remains, however, that an answer must be supplied. Therefore, man offers religion to satisfy the answer of God. Religion is the painting of a god who fits smugly into the back pocket like a magic wallet—conveniently satisfying.

But man is smarter than religion: he knows where to lay his faith and beliefs. Man knows it is impossible to disprove God even though there are no visible proofs. He also finds that it is impossible to discredit God because the acts of God make men tremble. It is therefore necessary to spend time researching and cloning the work of God to figure out the way to God. But man is smarter than himself. He knows his faith is the legitimate claim to the guaranteed promises of God even while it has no earthly evidence. Faith must stand alone: in God alone. So carefully, he measures his belief in God on his never-ending quest to prove God.

Take any of the impossibilities which history hails as acts of God, shed even the tiniest proof that they are true, and perhaps that would satisfy. Let science validate the Red Sea's parting or prove that the walls of Jericho fell at the blowing of horns. Greater still, God could indulge man's curiosity and remove the mystery of the Earth and time by allowing man to find Eden and its angels with the flaming sword of fire.

When science finds Eden, it will write the cure for every disease. When the rulers of the Earth touch the Cherubim of Eden, they will write the code that ends all wars. But man has been kept locked in the misery of his mind so that he never thinks of Eden, and if he does, the eternal truth of entering *The Way* is undesirable. *Now, lest he put forth his hand and take also of the tree of life, and eat, and live forever... So God drove out the man and placed at the east of the garden of Eden, Cherubim, and a flaming sword which turned every way, to keep the way of the tree of life.* (Genesis 3:24). If man finds Eden, he will live forever.

Adam was privileged to live in Eden and can therefore explain the difference between a body that will live forever and a body that is programmed to die. Today, the sons of Adam yearn for the taste of a body that will not die and for the mysteries of Eden. Did God leave any clues that would lead man back to the tree of life?

Listen to King Solomon, the wisest man, the man to whom the answer was revealed.

But I found him whom my soul loves: I held him and would not let him go. (Song of Solomon 3:4).

Behold, you are fair, my love, with doves' eyes within your locks. (Song of Solomon 4:1).

Your lips are like a thread of scarlet, and your speech comely. You have ravished my heart. How fair is your love, my sister, my spouse? (Song of Solomon 4:3, 9-10).

This is the beginning of a love dialogue and the interchanging of vows, which led to the intimacy of worship. Solomon found the One, the love of his soul, and began to express in mesmerizing language the intimacy that flowed between them.

A garden enclosed is my sister, my spouse: a spring shut up, a fountain sealed. Awake, O north and south wind and blow upon my garden, that the spices may flow out. Let my beloved come into his garden and eat his pleasant fruits. (Song of Solomon 4:12, 16).

Until the day breaks and the shadows flee away, I will get me to the mountain of myrrh and to the hill of frankincense. You are all fair, my love; there is no spot in thee. (Song of Solomon 4:6-7).

He likened this love to the love of women with the power to hypnotize the senses like a gushing fountain of life. He was married to an enclosed garden—Eden—and it contained a fountain of water that was sealed shut. To open the treasures of the fountain, he calls for the north and south winds to blow into the garden. He called for the winds to blow until the treasures of the garden were released, until the moment in time, the day, when the shadows of the promises were fulfilled because the fountain gushed open.

The Bible speaks of four winds of Heaven which God uses to blow upon the Earth, and each wind has attributes which are used to accomplish specific assignments. The north winds drive away the rain, and the south winds quiet the Earth. These soft winds were instructed to carry the myrrh and the frankincense that were to be poured out for the love who had no spot or wrinkle, or any such thing.

He found love, the fountain of living water, and called for the wind of the Spirit to blow onto the garden. He pursued the love of the One, that together they would come into the garden and enjoy its pleasant fruit. Who is the One that Solomon spoke of, who was so wise and beautiful, sprinkled with myrrh and frankincense, fair with no spot, and a fountain of living waters? Isn't He the Christ? The wise men of the east honored Christ's birth with frankincense and myrrh. Then the soft winds of time blew until, at His death, the Roman soldier pierced His side and out gushed the fountain of living water. Jesus told His disciples, "*I AM the way*—back to the Garden of Life." *So God drove out the man and placed at the east of the garden of Eden, Cherubim, and a flaming sword which turned every way to keep the way of the tree of life.* (Genesis 3:24).

Solomon saw it—in dreams, in visions, perhaps in his mind—but never came into the full experience of that which he saw. Imagine having a wish, a wonderful knight in shining armor who would come and whisk you away on his white horse. It may have started as a dream, but this dream became a wish of the heart. These thoughts roam around in the mind, haunting the soul, becoming larger than life. The desire for them pushes everything else in life out of the way, mentally building within the subconscious a hope, a dare, a challenge that must be solved. And then, *these all died in faith, without receiving the promises, but having seen them afar off, they were persuaded of them, and embraced them... And obtained a good report through faith. God provided some better things for us, so that those without us should not be made perfect.* (Hebrews 11:39-40). Solomon captured the vision of Jesus Christ mingled with the beauty of Eden, but never tasted the promise.

Jeremiah also entered into a vision and saw Christ as the fountain of living waters. *O Lord, the hope of Israel, all that forsake You shall be ashamed, and those who depart from Me shall be written in the Earth, because they have forsaken the Lord, the Fountain of Living Waters.* (Jeremiah 17:13).

Jesus spoke to the soul of the woman at the well, the woman who had five husbands and was presently working out the details of handling a sixth. Jesus brought answers and relief to her soul when He said, "I am the living water you need." *If you knew the gift of God, and who it is that says to you, "Give Me to drink," you would have asked of Him, and He would give you living water.* (John 4:10).

Here is the answer: the way back to Eden is a gift from God. Man does not need to prove anything to God, nor does he need to qualify for the gifts of his Father. All that man needs to have true life is to put a bridle on the desires of his soul, then give God no rest until He releases the *Fountain of Living Water*. There he will find the love that satisfies–the intensely passionate love of Jesus Christ.

John in Revelation pointed us to The Lamb when he said, *For the Lamb which is in the midst of the throne shall feed them, and shall lead them unto living fountains of waters; and God shall wipe away all tears from their eyes.* (Revelation 7:17). While the blinding tears are being wiped away, we enter into the love that is complete–a love without pain, a love that does not leave, a love that leads us to our Father God.

After testing and tasting every vice that has been hailed as the answer to living forever, man has come back to the drawing board to wrestle with the simple concept of *love*. Every vice must be rooted in relationship because the way back to Eden is based on a relationship of true love. Solomon, in his wisdom, caught a glimpse of love in a moment of forever. God sent His son, Jesus Christ, to lend a hand, to help man polish and perfect that love.

When man is submerged in the Fountain of Life and is purged in his mind from the soulish desires of the forbidden, he will live forever. Man must go back to the beginning and accept the terms of Eden in order to live forever. The contract of Eden simply states, "Refuse to feed your soul with death. Feed your soul with life, and you will live forever." When man thinks of living forever, he turns his thoughts to God and begins his bucket list of complaints. Halfway through the list, he turns his frustration to whether God exists or whether He is a myth. Then he craves proof of God, but that is foolishness in its perfection. If man were to find God, how would it be of any benefit to him? God cannot be molded into a puppet to be used conveniently. Instead, there should be a longing to be clothed in a body that is free from the guile of Lucifer.

It is time to dry our war-drenched battle tears and begin the search for the way, the truth, and the life. If living waters will quench the flaming sword of the mind, "Open up my soul and drink, enter into sobriety, and live forever."

CHAPTER

13

THE CORONATION

Every king that reigns in the Earth must have a coronation to legitimize his position. The coronation separates the man from ordinary citizens and elevates him above everyone. The affair is celebrated by his subjects, the people who will surrender their lives working to build his kingdom, his army, and his wealth. The entire domain—the people, the land, the food, the wealth—everything belongs to the king to do whatever he pleases. To reign as king is an enviable position, especially if the kingdom is wealthy.

Kings from centuries ago established their position by being ruthless because treachery and takeovers were common. The kingdom's protection was sustained by a well-trained, loyal army, and often the king was the fiercest soldier of them all. The wealthier the kingdom, the more likely it was to be attacked by neighboring kingdoms, who would punish the citizens with hard labor and taxes.

Kings were also the highest judges of the land, entrusted with the power to protect the kingdom internally and externally. The king's role was extremely vital to the longevity of the kingdom, and he had to be wise when choosing the leaders who served him. It was traditional to groom the king's sons to help protect the kingdom, and the firstborn was the rightful heir to the throne. However, the successor chosen to continue the legacy was the one on whom the king could lay his trust. This was the time and the season on Earth when Jesus, King of the Jews, was born, and ever so carefully, He shifted the culture around Him.

Jesus Christ is always referred to as the King of kings and Lord of lords; therefore, He had to outshine the kingdoms of all times. To do so, He used the least resources of any king and accomplished the revolution of the Earth without even establishing a home of his own. He never lifted a sword, never shed blood, and His military policy was to free those who were enslaved or imprisoned. His army was a group of twelve men whom He trained as disciples. To this day, He is known to have had unlimited resources of undisclosed wealth, yet His purchases were limited to food and the basic needs of life. He had an army, He had wealth, and Jesus gathered multitudes of subjects who faithfully followed Him wherever He traveled. Unlimited power used only for good.

Like all other kings, before He took the throne, He had to be crowned. To earn the title of King of kings and Lord of lords, Jesus was honored with four different coronations. Not only did He earn His titles, but He also achieved greatness which far surpassed kings before and after His reign. History records that some kings established empires, others built monuments like the pyramids, and the scholar, King James, translated the Bible to English. Each of Jesus' crowning ceremonies anointed Him to enter into a glory that far outweighed any other king or lord. Each coronation empowered Him to carry out His significant assignment.

As per the culture of His time, the success of His kingdom attracted furious enemies and His last coronation was brutal. This coronation took place in the royal judgment hall of Pilate, governor of Judea. At the hands of the Roman government and fueled by the leaders of the Church, He was crowned *King of Suffering* and *King of the Jews*. There is a twist to this coronation as it occurred twice, and the double occurrence is evidence that whatever is done on the Earth, must first take place in Heaven. *Your Kingdom come, Your will be done on Earth as it is in Heaven.* Jesus became the Passover Lamb sentenced to crucifixion on Earth by Pilate, while in Heaven He was slain as the Lamb of God.

And I beheld in the midst of the throne, and of the four beasts, and in the midst of the elders, stood a Lamb as it had been slain, having seven horns and seven eyes, which are the seven Spirits of God sent forth into all the Earth. And I saw and heard the voice of many angels around the throne, with the beasts and the elders numbering ten thousand times ten thousand, and thousands of thousands saying with a loud voice, "Worthy is the Lamb that was slain to receive power, and riches, and wisdom, and strength, and honor, and glory, and blessing." (Revelation 5:6-12).

And all that dwell upon the Earth shall worship the beast, because their names are not written in the Book of Life of The Lamb which was slain from the foundation of the world. (Revelation 13:8).

Jesus was also crowned by the Holy Spirit at the waters of baptism to take dominion of the spiritual throne of Earth. Adam was the first man to be sent from God and he carried a pure specimen of God's DNA. Adam fumbled the cup, spilled and contaminated the DNA, allowing his children to become carriers of cross-contaminated genes. Jesus Christ was the second man to be sent directly from God to carry the Father's DNA. Jesus' success produced a spiritual birth of children, unlike Adam, who was programmed to give physical birth. Spiritual birth requires every step of the journey to be sealed by the Spirit of God. Therefore, Jesus carefully followed the playbook handed to Him by His Father. Instead of using his powers for creative inventions, or, instead of sitting on a throne as a ruler, He humbly walked among the people, healing, teaching, and providing hope.

All who surrender to the doctrine of Jesus Christ become spiritual sons of God, infused with the DNA of God the Father. At baptism, Jesus was licensed to carry the miraculous power of God's DNA to man. The Holy Spirit descended like a dove on Jesus at His baptism, and from that moment on, miracles began. From this coronation, the word of the prophecy, *God is with us,* became a reality. The throne of Earth was now restored to God through Jesus Christ.

His first earthly crowning was at His birth, and the title given was *King of Glory.* The writer of Hebrews said, *When He brought the first begotten into the world, He said, "Let all the angels of God worship Him."* (Hebrews 1:6). This ceremony was celebrated by angels, shepherds, and kings. The story that is told places attention on a stable, which is said to be lowly and out of place for a king. However, to focus on the stable removes the focus from the destruction of the reign of demonic power that was forever broken. From the birth of Christ and evermore, the Spirit of God was given a legal spiritual contract to enter into the hearts of those who choose to let Him in. Through Christ, God came to man wrapped in flesh. God is not flesh; God is a spirit, but God hid Himself in flesh. Jesus was the Son of God, wrapped in flesh, and infused with His Father's Spirit, so man could have direct access to God. Jesus carried the pure spiritual DNA of God to the Earth so all who wish to access God can be anointed by the Spirit of God.

However, the greatest and most significant of His coronations took place on the Mountain of Zion in Heaven. This coronation was most troublesome. Man's existence, his knowledge, his ignorance, and his destiny were all birthed out of the first coronation of the only begotten Son of God. The choice to elevate Jesus above the rest of the angels, making Him *God's Only Begotten Son,* sparked a rage of jealousy so tumultuous, it set the Heavens and the Earth on fire.

The Bible tells us that Lucifer was chosen as the Son of the Morning, but second place was an insult to the beast. When God made the Holy Declaration (if He were an earthly king, it would be considered a royal decree), *You are My Son, today I have begotten You, O Son of My inheritance;* it was too much for Lucifer. Not only so, during the coronation, God lavished favors, possessions, and power on His chosen son. Jesus became the right hand of God's power, with authority to do all that was in His heart.

Jesus' rise to the right hand of the Majesty on High ignited the flame of betrayal in Lucifer, and he began to plot against God. He broke his covenant with God and ripped the cord of love that bound him to God. Then he gathered those whom he could convince to do the same to form an army against God and His son. *Let us break their bands asunder and cast away their cords from us.* God threw the entire gang into confusion and cast them out of Heaven. The torture and the distress that Lucifer and his gang suffered is the torment that man feels when they enter into man's presence. Lucifer's DNA is drunk with the poison of revenge, and he serves up the poison as an alternative to God for all who dine at his table.

Like kings of the Earth, those who have chosen to serve the Lord will be separated from their peers and elevated to positions of greatness. However, those who choose to be faithful to the Almighty God are destined to pay a painful price far beyond their imagination. But pain is purpose because the long-suffering of God is salvation. Those who are diligent use pain to profit. Whatever is thrown at man from the spirit realm does not only contain obstacles; every obstacle is loaded with purpose and profit. Those who fear the attack never open the package.

Lucifer, in his bitter jealousy, attacks everyone who is consecrated to God. During these attacks, God, in His sovereignty, usually remains silent. Those who have consecrated themselves to serving the Lord are warned of the severity of the test. They also know that woven into the cost of consecration is God's unfailing love and protection. The faithful yield themselves to be buffeted by the evil one and wait for the incomparable moments of beauty which are sent from God to strengthen their faith. For example, Jesus' birth into the Earth was a spectacular lighting show as angels filled the sky with radiance and song. There was also the moment of transfiguration where Jesus entered into the bliss of Heaven while He was still on the Earth. This was the moment when Jesus' body was strengthened for the crucifixion. Every step of the way, the Father is invested in the well-being of His sons because the price of the sacrifice is steep.

God will not abandon His children to evil. Jesus came to the Earth to prove to us that God the Father loves us. To prove the love, Jesus, the Only Begotten Son of Heaven, was slain for the sons of Earth. The Father must have paid the ultimate price to crucify The Beloved. He could have chosen a sacrifice that was worth nothing, but He demonstrated that man was as valuable to Him as His Beloved Son. The script was a masterpiece written in Heaven and published on Earth. The Lord, the God of all flesh, offered His Beloved Son, who denied His sovereignty and subjected Himself to being brutally slaughtered so that man would not be subjects of the torment and pain of evil.

KING OF THE PIT

God should have painted a dark, ugly, dismal picture of the angel who desecrated the treasures of his heart and wreaked havoc with His creation. Punishment for blasphemy of that magnitude should have held precedence for eternity. Yet, it seems the opposite is true. God did not have a meltdown, nor did He get angry. Instead, God gave Lucifer his own kingdom with power to rule, and Lucifer became King of the Pit.

The first account God gives of Lucifer in scripture is his use of the serpent's body in the garden of Eden to deceive Adam and Eve. Lucifer entered into the snake and used its voice to communicate with Eve.

Now the serpent was more subtle—crafty, shrewd, sensible—*than any beast of the field which the Lord God had made.* (Genesis 3:1).

This account reveals that Lucifer's strength is his ability to reason out a matter until he persuades the victim to report black as white. He targets intellectual brilliance using his favorite game, Hide and Seek. His foolproof strategy is to sell the mysteries of the spirit world to the mind of the seeker at the cost of the soul. Unknown concepts intrigue the mind and Adam got trapped in the thickets of the unknown. God waited until the encounter was over to visit with Adam. He knew it was only a matter of time before his children would have to face the tempter and make the choice between good and evil.

Now the serpent was more subtle than any beast of the field which the Lord God had made. And he said unto the woman, "Yea, hath God said you shall not eat of every tree of the garden?"

And the woman said unto the serpent, "We may eat of the fruit of the trees of the garden, but of the fruit of the tree which is in the midst of the garden, God said we shall not eat of it, nor shall we touch it, lest we die."

And the serpent said unto the woman, "You shall not surely die, for God knows that in the day you eat of it, then your eyes shall be opened, and you shall be like gods, knowing good and evil."

And when the woman saw that the tree was good for food, and that it was pleasant to the eyes, and a tree to be desired to make one wise, she took the fruit and did eat, and gave also unto her husband with her, and he did eat. And their eyes were opened, and they knew that they were naked, and they sewed fig leaves together and made themselves aprons. (Genesis 3).

A simple exchange of information. A pause to listen, to discuss ideas, opinions—there is no harm in intellectual banter. The creativity of the mind was intended to reason and debate the logistics and practicalities of any matter. In fact, cognitive dialogue stimulates the senses. Exactly! The perfect trap had been set for Eve. She did not know that God's rules are not suggestions to be toyed with or opinions for dispute. God's words are law, and God's laws are never to be broken.

And they heard the voice of the Lord God walking in the garden in the cool of the day: and Adam and his wife hid themselves from the Presence of the Lord God among the trees of the garden. (Genesis 3:8).

The judgment of God was not yet pronounced on Adam and his wife, they were still in a state of spiritual awareness. They possessed a spiritual body that could still hear the voice of God walking because God had not yet removed His Presence from them. Man, trapped in sin of the worst kind, is not deemed guilty until a sentence is passed. The first court case of the land was about to commence. Adam and Eve would be given an opportunity to appear in court and explain the details. The hearing would weigh the evidence and decide if they possessed sufficient knowledge to see beyond the offer and resist. However, because they had already pronounced themselves guilty, they heard the voice of God walking and hid themselves.

And the Lord God called unto Adam and said unto him, "Where are you?"

And he said, "I heard Your voice in the garden, and I was afraid because I was naked, and I hid myself."

And God said, "Who told you that you were naked? Have you eaten of the tree that I commanded you not to eat?"

And the man said, "The woman whom You gave to be with me, she gave me of the tree, and I ate."

And the Lord God said unto the woman, What is this that you have done?

And the woman said, "The serpent beguiled me, and I did eat."

And the Lord God said unto the serpent, "Because you have done this, you are cursed above all cattle, and above every beast of the field. Upon your belly shall you go, and dust shall you eat all the days of your life. And I will put enmity between you and the woman, and between your seed and her seed. A child from her shall bruise your head, and you shall bruise his heel."

To the woman, God said, "I will greatly multiply your sorrow and your conception. In sorrow you shall bring forth children. Your desire shall be for your husband, and he shall rule over you."

And unto Adam God said, "Because you have listened to the voice of your wife and have eaten of the tree of which I commanded you not to eat, cursed is the ground because of you. In sorrow shall you eat of it all the days of your life. Thorns and thistles shall it bring forth to you, and you shall eat the herb of the field. By the sweat of your face shall you eat bread, till you return to the ground, for out of it you were taken. Dust you are, and unto dust you shall return. (Genesis 3).

Dotted throughout the scriptures are events of Lucifer meddling in the affairs of men. The sons of Aaron, the High Priest, offered strange fire upon God's altar and died. In the life of Job, Satan approached God and asked permission to make Job's life miserable. King David had a vision of Lucifer conspiring against the Son of God. All these writings show the devious character of an angel who will stop at nothing to steal a soul. However, the narrative changed in the writings of the prophets Ezekiel and Isaiah. They captured the radiance and beauty of Lucifer as Son of the Morning.

Son of man, begin a lament... for this is what the Lord God says, "You were the seal of perfection, full of wisdom and perfect in beauty. You were in Eden, the garden of God. Every kind of precious stone covered you: sardius, topaz, diamond, beryl, onyx, jasper, sapphire, emerald, carbuncle, and gold. The workmanship of your timbrels and of your pipes was prepared in you on the day that you were created." (Ezekiel 28:12-13).

"You are the anointed cherub that covers, I have made you so. You were on the holy Mountain of God. You walked up and down in the midst of the stones of fire." (Ezekiel 28:12-14).

"You were perfect in your ways from the day that you were created until wickedness was found in you. Through the abundance of your trade, you were filled with violence, and you sinned. Therefore, I will cast you out disgracefully from the mountain of God, and I will destroy you, covering cherub, from the midst of the stones of fire." (Ezekiel 28:16).

"Your heart became proud because of your beauty. For the sake of your splendor, you corrupted your wisdom. So, I threw you down to the Earth and made you a spectacle before kings. You polluted your temple by the magnitude of your iniquities and by your dishonest trafficking. Therefore, I will bring fire from within you, and it shall consume you. I will reduce you to ashes on the Earth in the sight of everyone watching you." (Ezekiel 28:17-18).

"All those who know you among the nations are appalled at you. You have become an object of horror and will never exist again." (Ezekiel 28:19).

Hell from beneath is moved for you to greet you when you arrive. It stirs up the dead for you, even all the rulers of the Earth: it has raised up from their thrones all the kings of the nations. (Isaiah 14:9).

They all respond to you, saying, "You too have become as weak as we are; you have become like us! Your pomp is brought down to the grave along with the music of your harps. Maggots are spread out under you, and worms cover you." (Isaiah 14:10-11).

How have you fallen from Heaven, O Lucifer, Son of the Morning? How are you cut down to the ground, you destroyer of nations! (Isaiah 14:12).

For you said in your heart, "I will ascend into Heaven, I will exalt my throne above the Stars of God. I will sit also upon the Mountain of Zion, in the sides of the north. I will ascend above the highest clouds, and I will make myself like the Most High." (Isaiah 14:13-14).

Yet you shall be brought down to Hell, to the sides of the pit. Those who see you shall narrowly look at you; they will look closely and say, "Is this the man who caused the Earth to tremble, who shook the kingdoms, who turned the world into a wilderness, who destroyed its cities and would not release the prisoners?" (Isaiah 14:14-17).

All the kings of the nations, even all of them, lie in glory, everyone in his own house. But you have been cast out without burial, like an abominable branch, like the garment of those who are slain; thrust through with a sword, who descend to the rocks of the abyss like a carcass trodden under feet. You will not join them in burial because you destroyed your land and slaughtered your own people. The offspring of evildoers will never be remembered. (Isaiah 14:18-20).

Could it be that time holds in its cards the possibility that all who sinned could repent—those who sinned in weakness and those who sinned deliberately? Could it be that Lucifer and his angels are unaware that time has been given so they too could repent and get back in favor with God? It may be safe to say that man is mostly ignorant of the truth of God and the true path to repentance. The responsibility to protect the soul is given to each individual, but without a true understanding of how the process works, the soul will eventually die. Lucifer continues to work overtime to steal the souls of men, but what would happen if he turned his heart to God and spent his days in repentance? What would happen if Lucifer repented?

It would be unjust of God not to state the punishment He has prepared for those who choose not to repent. The penalty is a lifetime membership in a state-of-the-art furnace ruled by a king whose love language is torment. But God's judgment for man is not swift. God likes to reason and discuss matters, so He has an open invitation for man to visit and get to know Him—anytime. Time is God's justice.

... and I saw the beast, and the kings of the Earth, and their armies, gathered together to make war against Him that sat on the horse, and against his army. And the beast was taken, and with him the false prophet that wrought miracles before him, with which he deceived them that had received the mark of the beast, and them who worshiped his image. Both were cast alive into a lake of fire burning with brimstone. (Revelation 19:19-20).

And the devil that deceived them was cast into the lake of fire and brimstone, where the beast and the false prophet are, and shall be tormented day and night forever and ever. And I saw a great white throne, and Him that sat on it, from whose face the Earth and the Heaven fled away; and there was found no place for them. (Revelation 20:10).

And I saw the dead, small and great, standing before God; and the books were opened, and another book was opened—which is the book of life. And the dead were judged out of those things which were written in the books according to their works. (Revelation 20:12).

And the sea gave up the dead who were in it, and death and hell delivered up the dead who were in them; and they were judged, every man according to their works. And death and hell were cast into the lake of fire. This is the second death.

And whosoever was not found written in the book of life was cast into the lake of fire. (Revelation 20:13-15).

The end, for the King of the Pit.

CHAPTER

15

THE JUDGE OF ANGELS

Take your measuring pen and begin charting the news of the world we live in. Quickly, you will conclude, no matter how optimistic yo choose to be, that the world is deeply wounded, and her pain is great. How is it possible that so many people live troubling lives every day? After thousands of years, shouldn't man have learned and perfected the art of happiness, and health, and prosperity?

Shall we come to the soft conclusion that someone or something is responsible for the continued injustice in our world? It cannot be that man is the master of his own demise when the pain he experiences is so overwhelming. The truth is, he is the victim, trapped by an invisible wound of the heart which controls and leads him to his recurring defeat. The wound cannot be cured by being realistic, or by acts of fairness, or justice because the wound is spiritual. As he searches for answers to life, man tends to drift towards creative solutions that disrupt his connection to Heaven. The further he pulls away from God, the further he drifts from peace, joy, and happiness. His lack of connection to Heaven is the breeding ground for trouble.

We should agree that it is a fair assumption to believe that God is responsible for the disorder. After all, He is God, and there is no other god that compares to or can be likened unto Him. God rules supremely and sovereignly with complete autonomy. No one nor anything that exists or will exist will be able to interfere with or interrupt the sovereignty of God. Yahweh, the creator of Heaven and Earth, is absolutely and solely responsible for every nano detail of every life that has entered or will ever enter this world.

However, God does not have full authority in the Earth. God created the Earth and, by rights and privilege, is the titled owner; but in an irrevocable contract, God deeded legal guardianship of the Earth over to man. This is a business transaction—God owns the land but has leased the property to man. *The Heaven, even the Heavens, are the Lord's, but the Earth He has given to the children of men.* (Psalm 115:16).

Presently, God's only legal power in the Earth is that of the creator. Additionally, when God decided to hang the Earth in space, darkness was already present and God allowed the darkness a fair shot at roaming the Earth.

In the beginning, God created the Heaven and the Earth. And the Earth was without form, and void, and darkness was upon the face of the deep. (Genesis 1:1-2)

Again, there was a day when the sons of God came to present themselves before the Lord, and Satan came also among them to present himself before the Lord. And the Lord said unto Satan, 'From where have you come?' And Satan answered the Lord and said, 'From going to and fro in the Earth, and from walking up and down in it.' (Job 2:1-2).

The Earth is like a property that is overrun with weeds of evil instead of being developed for its proper use. The leaseholder is the only one legally qualified to clear the land and develop the property. Anyone who comes onto the land without an invitation is trespassing, and it is no secret that trespassers are prosecuted. Darkness was present before time began, but darkness was not given jurisdiction in the Earth. Whenever evil presents itself, it is a violation of human rights. Yet, evil has become so bold, it is not satisfied with trespassing and squatting on the land, it also takes up residence in the heart. The feelings of depression, and anger, or hopelessness are evidence that evil is having lunch in the heart. Where is the sign that says, 'no parking'? Man is not the creator of the trouble. Man is the puppet of demonic angels who trade the souls of men by trickery, eager for a moment to rule on the Earth.

The players of the Earth are God the creator, evil as a bystander, and man the leaseholder. Man stands at the center of the plot, surrounded by the decision to choose good or evil. Even worse, he is far outweighed by angels who are greater in strength, knowledge, might, and power. The question surfaces, "Did God draft an ingenious design for this Earth-and-creation story which has not yet been discovered?"

To stage the defeat of man, evil converges on the Earth with its hosts of fallen angels, called 'demons'. The rules of the game never change: man must give consent before angels can use their powers. However, demons are master manipulators and worm their way into the hearts of men with all kinds of lies laced with enticing offers. Ignorance or blindness of heart are the famous cards of defeat dealt by the hand of evil. In fact, more souls have been taken out by not knowing or understanding that they were trapped in darkness.

This is a frustratingly tangled web where man is the blindfolded, manipulated, weakened, trapped, wounded, and hurting victim. Angels are greater than men in strength, where strength equals knowledge, might, and power; but there is one piece of the puzzle that is yet to be laid on the table. Available to man is the wisdom of God. Wisdom is the gift of the mind of God that must be used to destroy the unseen manipulative foe who destroys by trickery.

Every battle that has been won—spiritual battles, physical battles, military battles, battles in man's dream—wisdom was the tool that decided the victory. When God handpicks a leader, He equips him with the Spirit of God: with all manner of wisdom, understanding, and knowledge. Those who partake of God's Spirit become rulers of angels.

Know you not that we shall judge angels? (1 Corinthians 6:3).

He who is spiritual judges all things. (1 Corinthians 2:15).

Men, through the Spirit of God, become judges in the heavenly realm. Judges are interpreters and upholders of the law. Those who do not abide by the tenets of the law are sentenced to punishment. When a judge pronounces a sentence, he does so by correctly applying the rule and the effects of the law. Thus, Jesus told Peter he had the authority to chain spirits in the Heavens. By understanding and applying spiritual law, man commands that which should be held in chains. He can bind the spirits in the heavenly realm or loose them as they deserve. Man walking in the wisdom of the Holy Spirit is a judge in the Heavens. Just as the evil enters into the Earth and plays his hand, so God has made His children spiritual judges who are empowered to enter the Heavens and spoil the evil.

And I will give unto you the keys of the kingdom of Heaven. Whatsoever you shall bind on Earth shall be bound in Heaven, and whatsoever you shall loose on Earth shall be loosed in Heaven. (Matthew 16:19).

No man can enter into a strong man's house and spoil his goods, except he will first bind the strong man; and then he will spoil his house. (Mark 3:27).

When a strong man, armed, keeps his palace, his goods are in peace. But when a stronger than he shall come upon him and overcome him, he takes from him all his armor in which he trusts and divides his spoils. (Luke 11:22).

Not only is there authority to sentence the evil spirits, but there is also power to destroy them with the sword. Man is given a sword for spiritual battles. After he has judged the angels worthy of destruction, he wields the sword in judgment. The sword of the Spirit is the word which he hears from the heart of God. God speaks, man echoes the word from God, and angels are judged and punished according to the word from God.

And take... the sword of the Spirit, which is the word of God. Praying always in the Spirit, and watching in the Spirit with perseverance. (Ephesians 6:17).

In the Book of Mark, there was a man living among the tombs, crying and cutting himself daily. Jesus went in search of the man and commanded the demons to let him go. When the people of the town witnessed the healing of a man whom they thought was beyond help, it frightened them. Miracles are merely God's power to control the evil spirits let loose in the Earth. Miracles reverse the activities of darkness. Spiritual authority passes judgment on the evil, so they can no longer lay their weight and power on man.

Jesus' mission on Earth demonstrated that God has given man power over angels. The gospel writers go to great lengths to document the lecture Jesus gave to his disciples as He gave them power over devils. They had returned from their mission and were excitedly reporting how the devils were subject to them.

And the seventy returned with joy, saying, "Lord, even the devils are subject unto us through Your Name." (Luke 10:17).

Wise men rule angels. When purpose is withheld from a man for too long, he will either roll over and die, or he will rise up and destroy the spiritual strongholds that stand against him. The first legal right given to man by his Creator, is the right to prosper. The first words spoken to Adam were, *Be fruitful, multiply, replenish the earth, and subdue it.* The code language, or rather, the spiritual language in this law is man's authority to devise the strategy to rule angelic darkness. We do not need to repeat the sins of our fathers. Adam failed in the law of prosperity because he took a shortcut to fruitful, multiply, and subdue by eating the fruit of lies.

The most captivating stories in life are those where defeats of the worst kind are turned into victories. Zechariah, one of the prophets of ancient Israel, saw the High Priest covered in sin. In the vision, he also saw the power of evil beside the priest.

"Satan, I rebuke you. I cancel your power against Joshua, My High Priest." The Lord stood from His throne, annoyed at the accusations coming from the evil one.

The Lord was ready to build up and prosper His land again and to give relief to His people from the burdens they carried. To make the land beautiful, He had to pluck the High Priest out of the spiritual fires that surrounded him. Not only so, the Lord had to defend the High Priest, telling Satan, "It does not

*matter to Me that you have tangled him in your web. He be-
longs to Me. Let him go."*

*"Angels, take off the filthy clothes the Priest is wearing."
The command from the Lord was urgent.*

*"Joshua, My Priest, this day all your sins are removed from
you, and I am re-dressing you from the Heavens." The gentleness of the Lord made the Priest bow in worship.*

*Zechariah, watching the spiritual change that God was be-
stowing on this chosen priest, cried out, "Please, put a crown
of authority on his head. Place a crown of purity on his head
so he will lead with the wisdom of the Almighty."*

*It was done. The High Priest was dressed and ready for the
Presence of the Lord. It was now time to restore him to the
power of the office of the High Priest. The angel read the
proclamation from the Lord.*

*Thus saith the Lord of hosts, "If you will walk in God's ways,
if you will keep God's charge, then, O Priest of the Most High
God, you shall judge God's house and keep God's courts. And
I, the Lord God of Heaven and Earth, will give you the understanding, and the authority, and access to walk among these
angels that surround you."*

There is a mystery that man must solve. He is to find the
secrets of God and use that knowledge to defeat the angels
of the dark world. No longer does man have to point his finger at God, nor does he have to be a victim of his circumstances. Man does not have to live in the shadow of pain and
death anymore. The verdict has been issued, man is empowered to rule angels.

DRAW YOUR SWORDS

Everyone was on edge, huddled in the spiky, jagged rocks amidst the darkness. All that could be seen were their fiery red eyes of defeat filled with hate, and the burning flames of evil that flowed from the belly of their leader. They had been drawn out of paradise by a mighty force, so great, it blew their minds. Swoosh! It was faster than light. Everything they had ever known—beauty, comfort, radiance, light—gone in a flash, forever.

They were not given the option to ponder the details of the war. Their minds were transparent to Lucifer, and to think would be to regret—they could not afford to play the fool, not now. He had tricked them into joining him; but they had to face the truth, they were hungry for power. He was pacing up and down, back and forth, madness oozing from his veins. Everyone knew he was looking for someone to take the fall for the failed plot, so they were all deathly quiet.

Death began to stir, but Lucifer stared him down. It took him a moment, but he raised his ugly head again, this time with words of comfort.

"Mighty one, think of the greatness of your achievement. No one will ever be able to attain the eminence you have. You have demonstrated power equal to that of the great God. You have become like God. Instead of focusing on what we lost, we should celebrate what we have achieved."

The room erupted in cheers. Lucifer halted in mid-air and the sulfur from his monstrous breathing began to subside. Death saw that he had made an enormous impact, so, putting on a grin, he continued his assessment.

"You have become a god."

The demons began shouting. The noise was so great, there was no distinction between what was being said. On the north corner, a fight broke out and began spreading like wildfire. Death bounded in the air and threw a blanket over the turf—instantly, the room was quiet.

"As I was saying, your majesty, through your intellectual brilliance and your military prowess, you have single handedly created an eternal kingdom. You are the great one."

Whistles and cheers rose from the crowd, and this time it was clear they were celebrating their leader. The icy blanket of death still covered the brood in the north corner and no sounds were heard from them.

Not to be outdone, and because he needed his share of the spotlight, Hell cleared his throat to take the floor. "All is not lost. The war is not over. God lost His mind when He consented to your plan to make the cowards pay. That, O most high, is our ticket to revenge."

Lies-n-Deceit had to seize this opportunity to be inducted into the top tier of gang leaders. He was ugly to look at and frail in stature, riddled with unsightly pockets of scum from multiple fights to defend his myths and fabrications of the truth. He had never held any position of importance in Heaven. This was the perfect opportunity to break the mold. He had earned his title as Liar during the takeover, where it was his job to come up with the perfect lies to convince all the angels to partner with Lucifer. He was partly successful because he rounded up quite a following. He could cover that failure with more lies and take a lofty position with this lot of misfits.

"Revenge is not complete unless the sword of our rebellion pierces the heart of God. God hates lies. Let me prepare the Book of Lies to feed His precious little ones."

Lucifer's dagger-pointed eyes put on a huge grin. He had truly collected an insidious bunch. He began to chuckle. This was not the time for his burning anger. This was the staging of a different kind of war. A war that would reduce God's Kingdom to nothing. He did not get the throne, but he had become a god in his own right with the deed to a third of God's property. Well then, it was time for a new strategy. He gave the *meeting signal*, and his hit-man Thief, and his confidante, Trouble, came bowing. He reclined on Thief, with one foot extended to rest on the back of Trouble. He could count on Trouble to bring him comfort in times of uncertainty.

"Death, remove your blanket; I need the participation of those despicable rejects." He began looking around, admiring the results of his brazen accomplishment, and the sulfur from his flaring nostrils began to fade.

Death turned to the north corner and grudgingly ripped the blanket, shredding the skin of those in its path, creating awful shrieks and screams. Annoyed, Lucifer wielded a strong back-hand blow, but Death expected the move and dodged the effect.

"Here's the new plan." Lucifer raised himself to address the crowd. His body entered into a state of calm, and his entire being began transforming itself into an angel of light. His heavenly beauty returned, lighting the blackness of the abyss and surrounding his troops with a false sense of peace.

The place was a dungeon of jagged black rocks, spiking into odd-shaped terrain as far as the eye could see. All of Lucifer's followers were wounded and bleeding from the fall. The pain in their faces was intense: none of them had ever seen or experienced that kind of trauma. Amazingly, all of them escaped with their swords—some broken or bent, and others charred. Sickness' handle was glued to his bleeding knuckles, but the entire blade was gone. It must have been a brutal fight.

It was the moment of consciousness where they could truly examine the cost of the war. A surge of pain from the reality of their failure started to permeate the air, and no one paid attention to Lucifer. There was no point in listening to the leader of failure. He had nothing more to offer; in their eyes, he was just an ambitious traitor. Secretly, everyone had withdrawn their loyalty, and no one had confidence in his conceited plans. The only thing that held them there was the fear of his torment. He was the king of torment.

A sickening rage of rejection rose up in Lucifer's flaring nostrils and the dungeon grew deathly black again.

"As I was saying," he shouted his words, trying to gain control. "We all have retained our heavenly powers. They will not have their power on Earth so we will sell at the cost of their souls." He was not connecting and he knew it, but he had to keep going.

"Our strongest gift is our power to deceive, and we will wrap every offer in the guise of prosperity. We know God's word is true; they will not remember us or the war; therefore, we will have the advantage of stealing their souls into our doomed eternity. Befriend them and rip their hearts out before they know it."

"Master, what shall we do about Michael and his team? Won't they come after us again?" It was Hatred, he was right under Lucifer's nose. Everyone knew to avoid him or feel the knife of his bitterness because he fights ruthlessly for position. His wounds could be seen by the fire oozing from Lucifer. He was hard to look at, charred on the left side with a missing right arm—the war really did him in. Before he accepted the call to the war, he was God's spirit of rest. Now, he was a misfit, spreading division and fear whenever he opened his mouth.

"They will be bystanders, available to help the cowards. We can transform ourselves to look like them and offer our help. Friends, this is not hard to do. One of the reasons we failed is that you are all seeking to rule. The greatest position you will have will come from combining your strengths." As his tone grew angrier, the darkness grew darker.

"You bunch of idiots; you did not follow my lead. We did not fail because it was impossible, we failed because you wanted power. Adolf, you and Stalin cost me this war. Stalin, you rose up to the throne of God without waiting for my signal."

"Adolf, you were supposed to attack Gabriel and intercept the messages to God. You fool, you wanted to keep the messages so you could take his position after the war. Dumb fool."

"I am assigning you to Abraham when he comes down. He asked for a lineage that would carry the truth. I want them all dead—massacred, starved, gassed—and I don't care how you get it done. Kill them all."

The room had become cold and thick with blackness from the rage of Lucifer's temper. Hell crawled forward, slowly starting a warm fire to pacify the rage of his master. With one swift blow to the chin, Lucifer sent him and the fire rolling into the abyss.

"You bumbling lot of fools. This is our last chance, and anyone, anyone who dares to fail will feel the wrath of my torture for eternity. We have been given an equal share of time. Our time to work is called night; we work under the cloak of darkness. Lie low in the daytime unless you have your hooks in your victim. Remember, force works temporarily; deception is our best tool."

"God has already started construction of the Earth; He is now on his sixth day. Today Adam will come down to Earth. Everyone will remain in the abyss until I take Adam. No one will move until I take Adam." Lucifer's gut began to erupt, boiling over with a stench so nauseating that the demons began to scatter.

"Deceive them, lie to them, destroy them—draw your swords and plunge them into the hearts of every man, then haul them off into the abyss where eternity is waiting." His shouts echoed into the caverns of darkness, where the fear of his venom made all who believed in him terribly afraid.

THE COURT OF HEAVEN

What would you do if the soul of the Earth were handed to you? Given absolute power over every created thing, how would you govern? Kings and rulers would be given special God-like privileges if they pledged to rule fairly. Man would never sin against his brother, and he would live in a world without pain, or lies, or evil. But the Earth is not in a state of perfection, so the sense of identity and knowledge of the Earth would also have to be corrected. The identity of the soul must be healed before there is order.

The soul of the Earth is in pain because man is a victim of his desires. God came up with the only solution—choice. Choice is not just the privilege of being impulsive; it is also accepting the results and outcome of every action. God, in his sovereignty, saw that buried in the DNA of some were irresistible desires for mischief. Therefore, He sovereignly designed an end game of lumping the good into their own basket, so those who were coded for trouble could willingly make their choice and eventually feast on the fruits of their own decisions.

However, He did not leave the matter entirely up to man and his cravings. Right from the beginning of time, God told Cain, the son of Adam, that he must become his brother's keeper. Beyond the lights, and glitz, and hype of the Church, or its seeming failure, is a powerful spiritual mastermind called *prayer*. Prayer is the right of every man to connect with God for help, especially in times of need. The Church has preserved that right and the Presence of God in the Earth with fervent diligence. When the priest says, "Time to pray," it means God is listening.

Every prayer brings man's petition into the courts of Heaven citing spiritual laws. Prayer demands, by the law, that the court of God issue a cease-and-desist order to the hateful works of evil. In prayer, man judges evil, not the victim who was used to commit the crime. As he bows his heart to the Almighty Judge, he is given understanding and truth. With this knowledge, he makes a case that cannot be denied: a case that lays the blame on the head of the evil. In prayer, he uses the law of forgiveness and mercy to bring healing to the one caught in the wrong.

The language of prayer focuses on laws that free the victim, while, on the other hand, they cripple the works of evil. The courts of Heaven wait to hear prayers that free those who were used to commit the wrong. The purpose of hiring a lawyer is so that the case will be strengthened by someone who knows the law. The spiritual lawyer goes into prayer not only to free the soul from the burden it carries, but also to cure the sin. Upon such, prayer demands that the true culprit be sentenced. Evil has violated every sacred right of man, but man has not taken it to task. Man continues to hesitate to enter the spiritual courts of prayer to demand justice.

No one with understanding leaves the courts of Heaven without knowing that the petitions were granted. The spiritual lawyer knows when the prayer has been answered because the court issues an order called *faith*. Faith becomes the document that opens the doors of justice over and over again, until release from the chokehold of evil becomes a reality. Imagine the power of those who enter into the courts of Heaven to fight for the wounded.

"Saints, this Court of Heaven is now called to order, you are hereby summoned to the hearing of Man versus The Accuser on the matter, Violation of Identity."

"All rise. The Court of Heaven, Holy Judicial Circuit is now in session. The Honorable Judge Chokmah presiding."

"Who brings an accusation against this life?"

"My name is Satan, a self-appointed accuser. The business of my trade is to find those who have breached the spiritual laws by which men should prosper. I bring before this court a soul lost in the thickets of worthlessness. I therefore claim that this soul, by virtue of a lack of identity, has given itself over to my control. I take full authority and issue the claim that this soul continues no longer in the Earth. My request is that you grant me the deeds and rights to its eternal destiny."

"Accuser, your argument is at best a request of confusion. Are you requesting that the soul be given to your eternal flames simply because the soul has been deathly wounded and healing may never be realized?"

"Your Honor, the protocols of spiritual law demand that before I make any approach to snatch the victim's soul forever, I must request this court's permission. Your Honor, you are of a wise and understanding heart, and you know very well that a soul which has been broken to this magnitude never recovers. Society has no use for these ill-used vessels, as they cannot contribute to the betterment of any. Souls like these are best suited for the abyss to continue the torture to which they are accustomed."

"We both know that to remove the soul from torture, and to bestow even the highest order of love, is a waste of time and energy. These indigent failures belong to me, my kingdom works best with the refuse of the world. I have worked hard to build up a following of fools. So far, we have succeeded in providing them comfort in their misery by a continual leveling up of additional confusion. Your Honor, it is just a formality to approach the court. You can save us precious time by granting me access to these on my list for the day. Here, I have put together a list of six hundred and sixty-six thousand for today."

"What is the name of your first victim?"

"Name, yes, name. I... I did not... I... I am not sure we identify them by the names you have in your docket. The names we use would not correspond. I would hate to tell the truth, but we really assign names based on how gullible the victims are to swallowing our lies. Therefore, this victim has been labeled 'Garbage'."

"What is your case against... Gar... I'm sorry. What is your case against this soul?"

"This thing is a mixed bag of troubles. Unwanted birth, lack of fathering, abandonment; and of course, this one has now begun to self-destruct, finding ways to keep the cycle going. Your Honor, please let me spare you the time and the valuable resources of this honorable court. I have put together a list of mentally broken souls who will never lift their heads to find the true meaning of life and eternity. It is just not in their nature. Allow me to explain it this way;

they are like a fruit that has rot in the core, not a blotch on the surface, but rotting from the heart, and they cannot be saved. Again, it would be a precious waste not to let me continue the inevitable."

"Please let me remind you that the Lord wastes nothing. OT Psalm Section 72, subsections 12 and 14, specifically states that pain of the soul is not wasted by the Lord. The law states that His children are precious in His sight. Please have each soul for which you are requesting custody brought to the bench so that the court may examine the true state of their condition."

Heads turned as the heavy doors creaked open. The list of victims trailed in, shackled and tormented. The court held its breath and the room gasped in silence. The pain and wounds could be felt, they were distressing, but nothing compared to the stench; the room smelled like death.

The judge was overwhelmed and visibly shaking. It seemed like such a casual request on a list when the Accuser asked that all these be discarded to eternal doom, but the morbid condition of the souls could not be ignored. This black, cold-hearted ball of evil had racked up quite a following. Now, in her hands, she held their fate: she was chosen to hand down their final verdict.

She turned to the clerk. "Did these souls have an opportunity to enter the arbitration of prayer, to tell their story to the Lord or to ask for Divine legal intervention?"

"Ahh... a... I think they were held back." She fumbled through her documents as if she were searching for answers. "I, uhm, I don't think so, Your Honor." How could she tell the truth? They had no one to plead for them.

"Schedule an arbitration of prayer, please. Also, assign to this case a Spirit-filled defender who will sift through the process and find out why these souls were not given the opportunity to be represented with Godly counsel."

The judge paused for a moment, deliberating the best course of action. "Take careful notes as I am requiring specific answers to these issues, which must be addressed in arbitration."

"Did these defendants know they could break the victim mentality and find true purpose and meaning in life? Also, do they know the reason for which they were born?"

"Did they understand that the offer they accepted from the Accuser would cause them to be trapped in their minds: that they could never progress after accepting the offer?"

"Before they are brought into the session of arbitration, the lawyers must work on finding and ripping out the thread of the continuous line of failure, whether it be generational or self-imposed."

"Before returning to this court, I need a spiritual cleansing of the ear and the eyes, the vessels used to fill the body with lies."

"I also want each soul to be given the option to receive the Holy Spirit. While this cannot be enforced, it must be laid out clearly so each person understands the protection the Holy Spirit will offer against ever going back to the dungeon of the Accuser."

"Officers, I want each soul unshackled so they can return to normal function. They must not return to the Accuser's pit."

"Mr. Accuser, I issue a cease-and-desist order of your hold on these victims. Turn over the keys you have used to shackle them to this court. Every key, including the keys you have used to build up conflict in their minds, and the keys you have used to bind-up their souls."

"I am issuing a restraining order against you and all your associates. None of you should be seen within a thousand feet of these souls, or you will be bound and thrown in prison. Am I clear?"

"The order from this court is effective immediately."

She stood. "Court dismissed."

WHERE I BELONG

There must be an advantage to this business of being a citizen of Earth. The design and plan for creating the Earth could not have been in favor of the rule of darkness. It may be understandable that evil was given time to prove its theory, but full authority to run the Earth amuck—no. Absolutely not. In fact, every time the evil one pulls a dirty trick, he gets permission from someone whose mind he has poisoned. Evil has no earthly authority; instead, it uses a body, and that could be any body, because it does not discriminate.

It stands to reason that, as with any other profitable venture, there must be diligence worked into searching out the advantages of this real estate called Earth. This theory must have been tossed around by many because the Earth is a treasure trove of continued success. However, earthly success cannot be the advantage man needs because the treasures of the Earth are not eternal. Yet, Earth can become the most productive and rewarding season of man's eternal restoration. While on Earth, man must regain that which was lost in the war of Heaven. Used wisely, time on Earth will restore heavenly rank and intimacy with God. It may seem as if rank is just a badge of honor, but it is more a badge of placement. In the life after Earth, every spirit will have a place, a position, and a title; all wrapped in the relationship developed with the Almighty God.

Eternity will be organized into kingdoms, governments, and communities, just as it is here on Earth. God will select kings, and rulers, and leaders: and issue positions and titles. This will depend on the skill each person masters while living in the Earth. Placement is where man fits in the larger scheme of life and comes as a result of the stock invested into eternal values. Each man must set aside time for spiritual matters while here on Earth because it is the only way to secure his heavenly position and title. Earthly success requires attention to detail, creative designs, and thinking outside the box. However, eternal success demands attention to the learning and obedience of spiritual laws.

The secret to success is law. Laws are the codes and theories built into the foundation and the structure, which hold the building firm during a storm. The design of the building and each nut and bolt which hold the structure together, are laws that govern and protect it. The truth is, prosperity is natural for those who govern responsibly by the code of law. Yet success is more than just understanding and governing. Success is upholding the law because the law protects against the brokenness of failure. Success honors the details set forth within the law and uses them to create the masterpiece intended by the law.

The way to destroy the structure is to study the individual parts, the design, and the whole. Once the whole is understood, the individual parts can be reworked to create chaos. The scheme of the fallen angels has been to outwit man, using the laws of God against him. Evil is the law working against man. Diabolical evil is tricking man into using the law against himself—self-destruction. Hell has no laws: it is a broken system of failure which says, 'Do as you please, just do not follow *The Law*.' The degree to which the law is broken determines the level of chaos seen in the Earth. The more the laws are broken, the further the decline of morality and the greater the pain inflicted in the heart of man.

The enemy cannot win unless he inflicts pain. His strategy is to twist the laws, become the third wheel in relationships, and force men into chaos and poverty. All these schemes of Hell which drag men into sin, stir up emotional and mental pain. However, none of these have any effect until man takes the pain, straps it onto his back, and starts a journey of being stuck at the point of pain. Hell's famous playbook is called *The Law of Pain*. Chapter One is titled, Stunted Growth: Chapter Two, Self-Destruct: Chapter Three, Blindness of the Heart: and the list goes on. God came along, opened the playbook and poured it onto His Son, then sent the Devil to nail Jesus to the cross. All that pain, all the sin, every bit has been nailed to the cross of Christ. Anything that is nailed to the cross is forgiven. All who receive forgiveness are healed because healing is the gift from the cross. But a gift is of no value unless it is used.

The spirit realm operates on principles that cannot change and Heaven made the rules that govern the Earth. Break the laws of Heaven and life falls apart on the Earth. The laws are simple; laziness leads to poverty: wisdom is too high for a fool: without God's counsel the people fall into deadly traps: a great house is built by wisdom—these are some of the laws written in the Book of Proverbs. Rising early is a simple principle that governs the law of wealth.

Discipline is an act that governs the law of money. Where there is sickness, the law of health has been broken. Search out any aspect of life that produces pain, and at its core, a spiritual law has been violated. On the other hand, respect the law, and the law becomes the road to success.

Spiritual rules are like the ocean: full of treasures, beautiful to behold, unfathomably deep, and help to sustain the life of man. But the lifeguard sign is posted, and man dares not break the rules of the ocean or he will be washed ashore. Earth-made rules are breakable because they are enforced by man, but spiritual rules cannot be violated. There are no shortcuts, or sneaking under the radar, or falsified fictitious copies. The season of revolting against God's throne is over. There are two reasons why the plot of an overthrow or an attempt to defile Heaven can never be repeated. The first is that the blood which has been shed has secured every boundary of Heaven and has washed away any trace of defilement. God has cleansed and sealed His kingdom with the blood of His son. The other reason is that the first subjects of Heaven were created and placed there; they were not citizens of Heaven by choice. This time, God has made it clear that all who will enter the portals of this celestial bliss will only be accepted on the basis of choice. Filling out the application for eternity is a choice.

A huge weight is placed on the head of every man—the burden to secure his eternal future. He must quickly understand who he is, so he can determine where he wants to live when he enters eternity. The sooner he gains that knowledge, the more equity he can build into his eternal home. Further, to secure his position, the man must complete his earthly assignment. Here on Earth, his financial or mental status dictates his advantage for position. The man who cannot read or is born with physical disabilities is placed on the bottom rung of Earth's ladder and treated as more of a nuisance than a person. However, to be assigned an eternal position and title only requires obedience to God. All that is required of every man is that he humble himself before God and faithfully complete his assignment.

Man knows he is making a choice for eternity based on the one he chooses to obey, and obedience is tough on the heart no matter whom he chooses to obey. To serve God, man has to reject the stubbornness of his heart which takes the form of ignorance, selfishness, or pride. Those who draw near to God know they have found Him because of the peace and love which washes over the soul. Choosing to hate a brother takes a lot of processing in the mind, but so does the choice to love. However, the real choice is not whether to love or hate, the underlying choice of love or hate is Heaven or Hell.

Every man knows in his heart where he will spend eternity. Kindness in a man's heart is the Presence of God living within him. Violence and hate take guts, and need strong conviction. In fact, most violators need to numb themselves with mind-altering substances before being abusive. Abuse is unnatural. Love is the sweetness of having peace, especially in the face of disagreements. When man chooses to love, he is building his case to live eternally in Heaven and those choices are made every day.

We belong with our heavenly Father, God. We belong to love, and beauty, and peace. Man deserves to be loved. Beauty from God is the ability to exist in a creation without guile, a creation that is true to the nature of God and full of goodness and integrity. Imagine a home where man never has to experience pain or sadness—no loneliness or shouting, no anger or the hurt it brings. We deserve love, and we deserve to live with God for eternity.

SENTENCED TO GRACE

It was softer than the wind, gentle, and sweet. It had no form, was not visible, and moved at the speed of light. Every operation was done in secret; chains and shackles melted: wounds, broken hearts, and shattered minds restored with that caring touch. As soon as a deal was brokered, with the gentlest of love, it whisked its subject off, ever so tenderly, to a place of healing and safety. Its laser focus never missed a target, and every assignment was tagged for life.

The roles and the assignments for everyone were pieced and parceled right from the very beginning. Some were required to make great sacrifices, others were given burdens to carry. He took on the role of watching carefully for those who would be blindsided, dragged into the abyss, and chained to the rocks. He would not allow a tear to fall in vain; within a second He would capture each soul and wrap it in His abundant grace.

How could He abandon His children to the strength of darkness? He knew they were no match for the power He had bestowed on the Son of the Morning—that covering cherub whose gift it was to walk on the stones of fire. That cherub was also given divine knowledge of the fine points of protecting everything he set his hand to claim. It would not be a fair fight. Not to mention, by virtue of the rank the cherub was given in Heaven, the children would be subject to him. Now that this deceiver had perverted his power, the children had to have a door of escape from its utter darkness. He was the only one capable of protecting His children from the corrupt version of true power. He had no choice; He would make it His business to watch, to protect, and to rescue His children with the love of His grace.

God sat down on His throne and called for a book to begin rewriting the laws. He had sent down a book of rules with Moses, but now He recognized it had resulted in more harm than good. The evil one took the rules, twisted them into yokes of iron, then sold them to the hearts of His children under pressure. The children could no longer see the benefit of the laws and made decisions out of the pain inflicted in their hearts. Something had to be done, and done quickly. To rewrite the law, He had to offer a pure sacrifice to justify the holiness of changing the law. By His own rules, spiritual changes can only be satisfied by sacrifice; therefore, He would write this law in His Son. It was time to send His son Jesus into the Earth—so let it be written.

He began writing. Jesus will be a contagious carrier of grace. He will take His assignment of grace and pour it onto Jesus. He would still be the Master of Grace, watching over His children and rescuing them from evil, but Jesus will carry grace into the Earth and distribute it to every man.

As a sacrifice, Jesus will offer a pure amendment to the unchangeable works of the law. No, He will not change the law, He will add to the law. He will add grace as a partner of the law. Grace will be the spiritual value of the law where those who stumble at the law can be caught by grace. The *covenants* will still be there, and the *shall nots* will still be there, but grace will empower the children to reach into the Heavens. Grace will meet them and remove guilt so they may continue on to find His love and partake of His peace.

To return to His Presence, the children must become the image of the law, as everyone in His Presence reflects the glory and the peace of the law. He Himself is the law, so there will be no erasing of the law. This must be done because His enemy has twisted the law and swayed His children into disobedience—*the law of sin*. Grace now becomes the force that is stronger than sin. It is poured out in doses more plentiful than sin, giving the children power far greater than the power of evil.

Of course, there are those who will stumble at Christ, the carrier of grace. They stumble because the gift of grace He carries seems to give permission to break the law. Soon they will see that the gift of grace is the measure of love that brings the vilest sinner out of the state of darkness. Grace is love without condemnation, which leads to oneness with the law. That abundance of grace uses the power of forgiveness to strangle the power of guilt. When the salve of love and forgiveness heals a wound, it can never be reopened by darkness. That emotion will forever belong to the Lord.

"Jesus, this is the message I want you to preach, and I will demonstrate its effectiveness after the nails of the cross. The nails of crucifixion represent the authority which the evil one has to hold My children in a place of mockery and torment. Every blow which drives the nail in place on Your cross will be the limited authority of evil because the nail can only go thus far. When the blows are completed, every sin will have been nailed to the Tree of Life. Then out of Your lips will pour the Living Law of Grace, as You cry, *Father, forgive them.*"

"Sin is not stagnant, but neither is grace. Sin shows My children how to die, but the grace You carry will show them how to live. They will all be exposed to the choice to dishonor and disrespect their Lord. However, as they make the decision to become a sacrifice for the truth, sin will instantly lose its power, and grace will take over the body. Sin works on the flesh, so Jesus, I will hand over Your flesh to the evil one to be examined by death. So it is written, now let it be done." Go!

...

Fires danced across the abyss like a starlit firework lightening show. The demons were drunk with excitement. The fires of their pleasure illuminated the dungeon as they celebrated their unexpected, amazingly great fortune.

"We did it, we did it." Hatred was the loudest. He was chest bumping with all who would tolerate his foul smell, while trying to make his way to stand beside his victorious master.

"Are you sure you have the Son: the-e Son of God?" Doubt-n-Fear never seemed to be at ease about anything. His voice was shaky, and so was his dance. His dance was shaky because he walked with a crooked stick. Crooked because it matched his spindly leg, or perhaps he had no care that his attire was flimsy.

"Nailed, pierced, crucified." Lucifer's tone was bold with pride. He seemed to stand a little taller today and somehow there was a glow to his demeanor.

Lies showed up out of nowhere. But everyone knew he had an eye for center stage and made up elaborate stories to get into the spotlight. "That's the end of God's reign. The treasures He bestowed on His Son are in that body... in that body. Now all of it belongs to us. Master, you, you are..." His voice went from high-pitched instructive, to solemn and tender as he choked back the tears. "Master..." He dropped to his knees, sobbing loudly while peeping to see the reaction on Lucifer's face. "...you did it."

Rejection ambled his bloated body to the front, recklessly pushing others out of his way. He was short and stubby, with goblet ears and a nose for details. He stuck his crooked finger in the air with a warning tone, "Get the body, bring it down to Hell, we must raid it and get all the treasures of Almighty God." He was giddy with excitement, still curled up in a ball, but excited nonetheless.

"I took care of all of that. Hell and Death are escorting it into their den, even as we speak." Again, that tone. It was unmatched; perhaps Lucifer had never spoken in that tone before.

This magical stroke of victory spoke to the sheer genius and excellence of his leadership. He had been studying the plans of God meticulously and finally found the pattern. When the state of sin in the Earth rises to an intolerable level, God always sends in a man to cure it. He had succeeded in creating a band of outlaws when God sent Noah to wipe them out with the flood. He followed Abraham's children into Egypt and began corrupting them with witchcraft when God sent Moses to free them. He had an eye for David, king of Israel, but David dodged his third bullet by entering into worship. The third bullet missed David but went straight into the heart of his son, Solomon.

God's ways are predictable. He was there when the angels announced Jesus' birth. He thought Herod was successful at wiping out the Christ-child, but only time could tell. Lawlessness was running rampant when he visited John the Baptizer in the wilderness. It was John who announced that Jesus was still in the Earth.

Timing, timing, timing. There had to be a weakness to God, and this was it. What was God trying to prove by sending His son into the Earth? Whatever it was, he would light the fires of Hell under it. He knew that Jesus was the ultimate treasure of Heaven and he knew Jesus' mild-mannered character. He was not a fighter; that made a planned assassination easy. Jesus had to have convinced His Father that He could turn the stony hearts of men back to God. Seems as if the plan was to make men like the *Bread of God's Presence*, so that each man's heart would be an open tabernacle for God. That kind of deal would bring peace to the Earth; there had to be a quick interception.

He organized a meeting in the wilderness to make a plea deal, the same deal he offered to Adam—but it did not work. It was a little scary being face-to-face with Jesus in the wilderness, so he went easy on Him. The business of coming to Earth could have been to strip him of his evil powers or to wipe out his kingdom. He could not be sure, so he played it safe. For two years, he observed every detail and realized that the plan was to hand the power over to man, so man would destroy the kingdom of darkness.

He went into solitude to carefully plan the crucifixion. After studying the disciples, he found Judas, and Judas became his henchman. Thirty pieces of silver, that was all he wanted for the sellout. The priests and religious leaders were already eating out of his hands, but he had to keep an eye on Judas because he was as nervous as a wasp. He revealed his plot only to three trusted strongmen—Traitor, Betrayal, and Murder. Together, they guarded the plan of crucifixion, and what a victory.

"We have secured a kingdom greater than we imagined." He turned on his musical genius and broke out into singing...

"Every power of God is in that body.

Imagine what we will do!

We'll wipe out God and Heaven,

Then we'll come for you.

There'll be no Hell below us,

We will rule by the power of night.

Imagine all the people,

Giving us their lives?

There'll be no countries,

We will control, kill, or die.

We'll convert all religion,

Become gods all the time.

We'll have all the people

Feeding on their lives.

Now crown me the grim reaper,

But I'm not the only one!

Some day you'll join us,

And Hell will be as one."

The song caught on like wildfire. The tune rocked the caverns of the abyss with a sound so refined, it made the darkness come alive. Every demon was singing, spouting a victory that could not be denied. Lucifer himself was drunk with a power that was out of control. His eyes were glazed over with evil so pure, and his body was shaking with the narcissism of pride. It all turned out in his favor. Now that he owned the body in which all the power of God was deposited, he owned God. Now he could desecrate and destroy as he pleased. First order of business, chain God to the abyss. Lock Him away until further notice. He had to take some time to digest the future of all this power. The demons around him were wild with frenzy, singing out his new tune. This had to be the most historical day in...

Pow! A thunderbolt of light blew through the dancing demons. The sharp edges of rocks flew like daggers through the air, piercing the bodies of the drunken victors. Their fever of intoxicating pleasure was instantly punctured by excruciating pain. Lucifer's lower face was torn from his body, and his teeth went flying through the air. Out of the abyss rose the live bodies of men and women who had been sentenced to Hell, now free of the chains of death. Above them was Jesus the Christ, leading them back to life. He was robed in a glorious body and the strength of His power pulled them from the darkness.

It was the Spirit of God. Hell and Death had rolled out their chains to secure the crucified, lifeless body of Jesus to the whipping post in their dungeon, unaware of the fate that was waiting to unfold. Hidden in the tortured, bloodied, dead body of the Crucified One was the power of the Holy Spirit. No one saw it coming, no one expected it.

The Holy Spirit surged to life and quickened the lifeless heart of Jesus with a spiritual jolt of power. Immortal life welled up inside Him as He issued the demand, "I AM here for the keys."

The power struck the two monsters with a sudden bolt of fear, shocking their senses with numbness. Jesus reached out and yanked the keys from their necks, rolled them into a ball, and tossed them into Heaven. Leaving his two ene-mies pinned to the rocks intended for Him, Jesus and the Holy Spirit crossed the morbid divide, entered the burning lake of fire, and began breathing the gospel of grace.

Chains and shackles began to melt. Shattered minds and wounds heard their healing. Hearts began beating again with joy and peace. The Father's request was now complete. The Holy Spirit gave the signal, and Jesus nodded in reply. With a thunderbolt blast, they blew Hell wide open and walked out with those who were sentenced to grace.

CHAPTER

20

THE WEDDING

S he was sitting in the Sunday School room leafing through the pictures in the children's Bible. Her eyes were a gentle brown, perfectly set above high cheekbones, on a light, bronzed, orange-toned skin that was flawless. Her tiny feet were dangling back and forth above the floor in those black patent shoes and her frilly white socks. It did not matter that her dress was silken white with patterns of reddish-orange roses, she could have been in rags, and she would still have been, without question, the most beautiful girl in the room.

Sundays were his favorite days—the times he got to see the delight of his soul. He never stayed far from her, perhaps a pew or two away, close enough to hear her melodious tones as the hymns were sung. His mother seemed to notice his curious interest, and he could often sense the silent words she spoke with her smile as she observed the intensity of his eyes. His father had many duties to perform and never had the time to sit with the family. His sisters were engaged with their friends and had no care that his eyes were fastened to the little beauty with the long ponytail.

Years had passed, and his life had changed. He had received a most prestigious award at an outstanding college, and here he was, sitting alone at the lunch table. He was a brilliant scholar, yet life was not fulfilling. He should have chosen the hamburger because the pizza tasted like paper. He held up his head to rise from the table, and there, walking across the room, was the goddess of beauty, the girl of his dreams. Chills shot through his spine. His eyes squinted, then bulged, then squinted again. She was leaving. His throat began to swell, and low, unintelligible sounds bumbled from his lips. He heard himself say, "No, never again." Without thinking, he rose from the table to chase the girl who had lived in his dreams for as long as he could remember.

Life could not be more beautiful; he had convinced her to be his bride, and everything he could ever imagine had come alive. With this gorgeous work of art promised as his bride, he was strong and fearless, achieving everything he set his sights on. Obstacles that crossed his path were destroyed as he climbed higher and higher above his peers. He became invincible; life was a pot of gold, and he owned the mine.

The day had come, all things were ready. Everyone worked hard to put this wedding together. The chapel had been transformed into a garden of white colors, filled with a sense of peace, and graced with beauty. Family and friends were all dressed up, and there was that exciting tinge of nervousness that comes with seeing the bride. He was in the moment, standing at the altar, waiting... waiting... waiting for his bride.

His father tapped him on the shoulder, "Son, this is it. You have been waiting for this all your life."

He sighed nervously in response. He was more than excited, yet his confidence was a strange mix—a blend of uncertain anxiety and delight. What were the odds that this day would ever come? How many directions could life have taken them? They had parted company for years, but God chose to bring them to this moment, and now she would be his forever. As he anxiously waited to see her face, the anticipation began to be unbearable. She had to make this journey alone. He could not be there to protect her tender heart or to reassure her as she pondered her future filled with unknowns. What if she changed her mind or wandered off in another direction? No, he had to trust that he had proved himself worthy of her eternal love. He had done all he could. Now he had to wait right here at the altar, so the world would know that by her coming, she pledged to be his forever. The waiting was unbearable.

Finally, the organ struck up the note. Whoever penned that song should be placed on a pedestal. It announced to the entire world that she had arrived. His heart began pounding, and his body felt hot. Beads of sweat found their way to his face, revealing the dialogue that was dancing with his mind.

His father looked him in the eye. "Congratulations, son, you've chosen for yourself a beautiful bride, and I am proud of you."

He shifted from one foot to the other, not knowing what to say. The walk down the aisle seemed to take forever. Photographers were in the way, but he could see her in the distance; someone was tinkering with her dress. Her father's smile showed the strength of his approval as he held her hand with the gentlest grip of power. Friends and well-wishers in the pews seemed to be slowing her down, everyone wanting to say hello, waving and mumbling. Can't they tell she's on her way to him?

Her father paused, right there in front of everyone, his eyes full of tears, and kissed her hand. It seemed no one cared that she was on her way to him. These delayed moments felt so dangerous. Didn't they understand that every pause before she was given into his hand left her vulnerable and uncovered from the perfect bond of his eternal love? He wanted to walk down the aisle and just bring her to the altar, but he had to compose himself. In just a few short seconds, she would be totally his.

She was halfway there, and he could just make out her eyes, and as they found him, the tension left the room and his heart began to dance. Then finally, she was standing across from him, and he counted the seconds that remained before he would be holding her hand, forever. The music stopped, the priest cleared his throat and announced to the world that her father was to place her hand in his as a symbol that he was now the father who would take her into eternity. The rest of the ceremony was a dream. With a kingly passion, he embraced her love and recited the promises of forever–the vows of love that would never be undone.

...

This journey to the altar of love is the passage of every man as he returns to his heavenly home. Everyone must take this exciting journey of the crossing from Earth into Heaven. It is an exhilarating moment as man closes out the only life he has ever known to enter his eternal home. The bride is fashioned gorgeously as she makes her way to the groom. In that snippet of time, she is bombarded with intense forces of guilt and doubt, spirits sent to steal her heart. She must be stronger than the overwhelming sense

of unworthiness and ignore the thoughts and feelings of regret. All these distractions are designed to pull her off the
path, to turn her heart away from the One she loves—the
One to whom she is pledged.

Christ the groom stands with the Father God at the altar
of eternal commitment, anxiously waiting, looking onto the
portals of the path to the altar of His heart. He cannot influence the moment; the bride must be fully persuaded of
the strength of His eternal love. She must, for one last time,
prove to every spirit of darkness which wooed her heart in
life that she cares only for the Lord Jesus Christ.

This is the day when faith is rewarded. The bride sees the
face of the One she had given herself to in life, the One she
trusted only by faith. It is the ceremony of completely uniting with the One who loved and gave Himself for the treasure of her eternal life. The wedding announces to the spirit
world that the bride has defied every lie, every devious plot,
every conceivable trouble thrown into her path; and with
full consent, has chosen to make her Savior, her Lord, forever. The entry into eternity is a holy, spiritual wedding ceremony.

Earthly weddings are God's way of allowing man to enter
into the experience and excitement of holy, heavenly wedding ceremonies. Earthly weddings are a taste of the same
nervous anticipation Christ experiences as each spirit returns to God the Father. The bride must make the journey to
the eternal altar alone. In that moment, she is surrounded
by forces that will make their last plea for her soul, endeav-
oring to turn her heart away from the One she has loved and
served, the one she was betrothed to in life. The bride must
enter the portal of eternity with extreme confidence and
unshakable love for the Lord Jesus Christ. Tucked away in
her heart, covered and hidden beneath all the activities of

life, is a spot reserved only for her Lord. In those final moments, she strips away all the layers of her journey through life to reveal the deep, riveting love she has for her Lord Jesus Christ.

The groom, Jesus Christ, is the most powerful One in the spirit realm. He is the One on whom the Father has chosen to lay the weight of Heaven and Earth. He gave His life as a sacrifice for the bride, and He is the One who is sent to receive her as she crosses the threshold of life into eternity. The bride is not a woman in the sense of a female, because as she steps onto the portal of Heaven, she sheds her suit of clay and the beauty of her spirit is displayed. The spirit of man is now decked with the glory of God, a beautiful robe of honor, fit for the kingly ceremony.

Wives, submit yourselves unto your own husbands, as unto the Lord. For the husband is the head of the wife, even as Christ is the head of the Church and He is the Savior of the body. Therefore, as the Church is subject unto Christ, so let the wives be to their own husbands in everything. Husbands, love your wives, even as Christ loved the Church and gave Himself for it, that He might sanctify and cleanse it with the washing of water by the Word. That He might present to Himself a glorious Church, not having spot, or wrinkle, or any such thing: but that it should be holy and without blemish. For this cause shall a man leave his father and mother, and shall be joined unto his wife, and they two shall be one flesh. This is a great mystery, but I speak concerning Christ and the Church. (Ephesians 5:22-32).

And they came to John and said, "Rabbi, He that was with you on the other side of the Jordan River, the one you said was the Christ, He is baptizing, and all men are following Him." (John 3:26).

John answered them, "You know that I said, I am not the Christ, but that I am sent before Him. The bride belongs to the bridegroom but the friend of the bridegroom, who stands and hears Him, rejoices greatly because of the bridegroom's voice. This makes me full of joy. (John 3:26-29).

How appropriate that man's arrival in Heaven is the celebration of a wedding. Jesus stands at the altar of Heaven, waiting to embrace those who have suffered for Him, waiting to introduce them to His Father, and to welcome them into the joys of their eternal home. The wedding makes the bride an heir to the estate. *Heirs of God and joint-heirs with Christ. Because we have suffered with Him, we will also be glorified with Him.* As the Bride of Christ, man becomes heir to the promises God placed in Christ... *which things the angels desire to look into.*

Christ lives for this moment—the arrival of His bride at the wedding altar of Heaven, the portal of entry into the eternal. After all the sacrifices He has made, His greatest achievement will be to hand to His Father countless numbers of souls who trusted His heart and His plan of salvation. The wedding is the most exhilarating moment of life, when they who, through much tribulation, persevered and prepared themselves for the ultimate welcome, *"Well done, My good and faithful bride;* welcome back, *enter into the joys of your Lord."*

ABOUT THE AUTHOR

I have been studying the pages of the Bible for more than 25 years, searching for the hidden clues to the meaning of life. If God exists and His words are true, there must be proof of His existence. Man lives in a world where seeing is believing. The Creator must have left evidence of Himself; somewhere. My study has led to conclusive answers that will satisfy the nagging questions of humanity.

As a deep thinker, I often place my thoughts on paper. Those papers have lead to plays, poems, songs, teachings, seminars, radio drama, television interviews, and books. My next assignment will be to publish a children's book titled, The Acorn Dance. And the dance with words goes on, and on.

FINAL NOTE

*T*hank you for choosing to join the millions of readers who are intentional about their lives on Earth, and their eternal future. God has poured the grace of His love on your life, so that you will never again experience defeat. Remember, setbacks are not defeats and the Holy Presence of God will never allow you to fail.

Now, grab a hold of the truth and the secrets of the Earth, and run this marathon of Earth with determination. One day we will sit at the Marriage Supper of the Lamb, and our names will be called to receive the prize of the high calling in Christ Jesus, our Lord. See you there!

www.ingramcontent.com/pod-product-compliance
Lightning Source LLC
Chambersburg PA
CBHW060934120626
46557CB00003B/996